UNIVERSITY OF NORTH CAROLINA
STUDIES IN THE ROMANCE LANGUAGES AND LITERATURES
Number 125

A CRITICAL EDITION WITH INTRODUCTION
AND NOTES OF
GIL VICENTE'S *FLORESTA DE ENGANOS*

A CRITICAL EDITION
WITH INTRODUCTION AND NOTES OF
GIL VICENTE'S
FLORESTA DE ENGANOS

BY
CONSTANTINE CHRISTOPHER STATHATOS

CHAPEL HILL
THE UNIVERSITY OF NORTH CAROLINA PRESS

DEPÓSITO LEGAL: V. 4.629 - 1972

ARTES GRÁFICAS SOLER, S. A. — JÁVEA, 28 — VALENCIA (8) — 1972

CONTENTS

	Pages
INTRODUCTION	
Gil Vicente and the Court	9
The History of the *Floresta de Enganos*	10
The *Floresta* and the Critics	13
Analysis of the *Floresta*	18
Some Antecedents of the *Floresta*	46
The Linguistic Texture of the *Floresta*	56
Norms Guiding the Transcription of the Text	60
TEXT OF THE *Floresta de Enganos*	65
NOTES TO THE TEXT	103
BIBLIOGRAPHY	129

INTRODUCTION

GIL VICENTE AND THE COURT

For thirty-four years and under the patronage of two successive kings, Manuel I (1495-1521) and John III (1521-1557), Gil Vicente served as purveyor of entertainment for the Portuguese Court. His was not an age of art for art's sake.[1] His entire dramatic career, initiated with the *Monólogo do vaqueiro* (1502) and concluded with the *Floresta de Enganos* (1536), was guided by the need to please his patrons. All his plays were written for the Court, and many were expressly designed to celebrate particular festivals. It remains uncertain, however, to what extent the dramatist had to subordinate his art to prescribed requirements. Even if he had to, this was not incompatible with Renaissance practices. Though for a modern dramatist writing to order is not at all the same as writing to please oneself,[2] some Renaissance artists seem not to have felt that patronage violated their creative spirit: Michelangelo considered benificial the pressure exerted on him by Giulio de' Medici;[3] Ben Jonson never complained against his employer.[4] Edgar

---

[1] Laurence Keates, *The Court Theatre of Gil Vicente* (Lisbon: privately printed, 1962), p. 113.
[2] See T. S. Eliot, *On Poetry and Poets* (New York: Farrar, Straus and Cudahy, 1957), p. 99.
[3] Edgar Wind, *Art and Anarchy* (New York: Alfred A. Knopf, 1964), p. 92. Besides it is very likely that, without the relentless pressure of Pope Julius II, Michelangelo might not have reached the height of his creativity; see Kenneth Clark: "The Young Michelangelo," in *Renaissance Profiles*, ed. J. H. Plumb (New York: Harper and Row, 1965), p. 46, and Ferdinand Schevill, *The Medici* (New York: Harper and Row, 1960), p. 186.
[4] Stephen Orgel, *The Jonsonian Masque* (Cambridge, Mass.: Harvard Univ. Press, 1965), p. 7.

Wind asserts that "as a rule artists prefer patrons who fuss to patrons who do not care."[5] Fortunately for Vicente, King Manuel I was a patron who cared and who took pride in encouraging artistic endeavors.[6] True, the playwright occasionally put his talent in the service of his patron's policies; but there is no reason to suppose that he felt any reluctance to do so or that the policies themselves were repugnant to him. His position at the royal Court was also advantageous to Gil Vicente's theatrical development for another reason: it "enabled him to enrich his scene with large and small devices and properties."[7]

Such were the circumstances under which the *Floresta de Enganos* was composed and produced before a courtly audience.

The History of the *Floresta de Enganos*

According to the rubric that precedes it, the *Floresta* "foy representada ao muyto alto & poderoso Rey dom Ioam o terceyro deste nome na sua cidade de Euora. Era do Senhor de M.D.XXXVI. Annos." The colophon informs us that it was "a derradeyra que fez Gil Vicente em seus dias." There is no indication that it was an occasional piece intended to celebrate some specific event in the life of the Court, though it is a court entertainment. The place and date of its performance, as given in the *Copilaçam*, have never been questioned by any scholar, unlike those of other Vicentine pieces: it is known that the Court was in residence in Évora from December 1532 till August 1537,[8] and that Gil Vicente was in that city in August 1535 and remained there till the performance of the *Floresta* the following year.[9]

---

[5] Op. cit., loc. cit.

[6] See J. P. Wickersham Crawford, *Spanish Drama before Lope de Vega* (Philadelphia: Univ. of Penn. Press, 1937), p. 62, and N. D. Shergold, *A History of the Spanish Stage* (Oxford: Clarendon Press, 1967), pp. xxvii, 236, 545. Both writers contrast the lack of interest in the theater on the part of Charles V and Philip II with Manuel I's patronage of it.

[7] Ronald B. Williams, *The Staging of Plays in the Spanish Peninsula Prior to 1555*, Univ. of Iowa Studies in Spanish Language and Literature, No. 5 (Iowa City: Univ. of Iowa, 1935), p. 54.

[8] Anselmo Braamcamp Freire, *Vida e obras de Gil Vicente* (Lisbon: Rev. Ocidente, 1944), p. 319.

[9] Ibid.; see also Aubrey Bell, *Estudos vicentinos*, trans. António Álvaro Dória (Lisbon: Imprensa Nacional, 1940), p. 77.

The year 1536 proved to be a disastrous one both for the history and the literature of Portugal: it saw the establishment of the Inquisition in Portugal; it was the year of Garcia de Resende's death, and perhaps, though it remains uncertain, of Vicente's; but, above all, it was the year in which Vicente's muse was definitively silenced. [10] Moreover, this same year marks the beginning of the eclipse of the autochthonous Portuguese theater — which was to be succeeded, for a short period of time, by the Italianate theater or Sá de Miranda and Luís de Camões, and then, much more lastingly, by the Spanish *comedia*. [11]

Following the establishment of the Inquisition, the first Portuguese writer to suffer the consequences of censorship was Gil Vicente. [12] His work was censored not only in Portugal but also in Spain. [13] Compared to some of his other plays, the *Floresta de Enganos* suffered few alterations or mutilations. It is to be understood that real literary censorship did not exist at the time of the dramatist's death, [14] and that any action taken against his work was posthumous: the first Portuguese Index only appeared —in manuscript form— in 1547. Despite the fact that Vicente's work was affected by the Indices of 1551 (*Rol dos livros defesos pelo Cardeal-Infante Inquisidor Geral nestes reinos*, Évora) and the *Cathalogus librorum qui prohibentur hoc anno 1559*, Valladolid, the *Floresta* appeared intact in the *Copilaçam* of 1562, which was issued only after it had been examined "polos deputados da sancta Inquisiçam." [15] For the first time, the play appeared in the *Catalogo dos livros que se prohibem nestes Reynos e Senhorios de Portugal*

---

[10] Braamcamp Freire, p. 310.
[11] For an extensive discussion of the so-called "escola vicentina," see Carolina Michaëlis de Vasconcelos, *Notas vicentinas* (Lisbon: Rev. Ocidente, 1949), pp. 509-602. See also Luciana Stegagno Picchio, *Storia del teatro portoghese* (Rome: Ateneo, 1964), pp. 53-74.
[12] António José Saraiva, *História da cultura em Portugal*, III (Lisbon: Jornal do Fôro, 1962), 146.
[13] Ibid., p. 155.
[14] I. S. Révah, *Recherches sur les œuvres de Gil Vicente. I. Édition critique du premier "Auto das barcas"* (Lisbon: Institut Français au Portugal, 1951), p. 12.
[15] For an account of the extent of Inquisitorial action on Gil Vicente's work, the following may be consulted: Carolina Michaëlis, *Notas*, pp. 9-83, 565-96; Braamcamp Freire, *Vida e obras*, Ch. vii; and Saraiva, *História*, III, 146-58.

(Lisbon, 1581). Its second edition, in the *Copilaçam* of 1586, follows the modifications imposed by this Index; a collation of the two texts shows that five lines were entirely omitted and seven altered; minor omissions and alterations occur also in the rubric, the colophon and a stage direction.[16] In 1624 was published the *Index auctorum damnatae memoriae, tum etiam librorum, qui vel simpliciter, vel ad expurgationem usque prohibentur, vel denique jam expurgati permittuntur* (Lisbon), in which one reads: "na Comedia *Floresta de Enganos*, perto do fim, o que da ventura se diz, lease cautamente."[17] The same warning is repeated in the *Index librorum prohibitorum ac expurgandorum novissimus* (Madrid, 1747).[18]

After its first publication in the *Copilaçam de todalas obras de Gil Vicente* of 1562, under the personal care of the dramatist's son Luís Vicente, and its second in the *Copilaçam* of 1586, the *Floresta* next appeared in the Hamburg edition of 1834: *Obras de Gil Vicente, correctas e emendadas pelo cuidado e diligencia de J. V. Barreto Feio e J. G. Monteiro* (Officina Typographica de Langhoff), three volumes. This edition was based on a copy of the *editio princeps* found in the library of the University of Göttingen, but the editors took many liberties with the text.[19] The subsequent editions of 1843 (Lisbon; same editors) and 1852 (Lisbon, *Bibliotheca Portugueza ou reproducção dos livros nacionaes escriptos até ao fim do seculo XVIII*) are virtually the same as that of Hamburg.[20] In more recent times, the *Floresta* has been included in the following editions of Vicente's complete works: *Obras de Gil Vicente*, ed. Mendes dos Remédios, three volumes (Coimbra, 1907-1914); *Obras completas de Gil Vicente. Reimpressão "fac-similada" da edição de 1562* (Lisbon, 1928); *Obras*

---

[16] Braamcamp Freire, pp. 413-14. The specific changes will be pointed out in the textual notes.
[17] Ibid., pp. 456, 458.
[18] Ibid., pp. 461-62.
[19] Ibid., pp. 372-75; see also Carolina Michaëlis, *Notas*, pp. 481-84. Besides the Göttingen copy of the *Copilaçam* of 1562, there are five more known located in: the University of Harvard, the Palácio de Mafra, the Biblioteca Nacional (Lisbon) the Arquivo da Tôrre do Tombo (Lisbon), and the Palácio dos Bragenças (Vila Viçosa); see Stephen Reckert, "El verdadero texto de la *Copilaçam* vicentina de 1562," in *StPh*, 3 (1963), 55.
[20] Braamcamp Freire. pp. 373-76.

INTRODUCTION 13

completas, ed. Marques Braga, six volumes (Lisbon, 1942-1944); *Obras completas*, ed. Álvaro Júlio da Costa Pimpão (Barcelos, 1956); and, without mention of an editor, in *Obras completas. Contribuições para o conhecimento das obras de Gil Vicente* (Porto, 1965). The *Floresta* has never been individually or critically edited. There are only passing references to it in Vicentine criticism, which suggests that no critic has found it worthy of his attention.

THE *Floresta* AND THE CRITICS

"The primary understanding of any work of literature," claims Northrop Frye, "has to be based on an assumption of its unity. However mistaken such an assumption may eventually prove to be, nothing can be done unless we start with it as a heuristic principle." [21] The question of unity as the test of literary worth has come to dominate present-day critical methods. Not all literary works, however, lend themselves to the application of the same critical formulas. It may well be that the kind of unity found in one work will not be found in another, but this does not necessarily mean that the first is superior to the second. It simply means that there may be more than one interpretation of the term "unity". Questioning the validity of our notion of unity, Eugène Vinaver duly remarks that it is "a metaphor traceable as far back as the 16th century, but not beyond, and not entirely valid for the 20th. Our failure to realize this has caused us to overlook the very things that give life and meaning to medieval literary art and to much of our own." [22] Turning to a discussion of the medieval *ars poetica*, he doubts whether "the implied notion of unity as something which cuts the work off from any other matter would have appealed to any writer of consequence in the last centuries of the Middle Ages;" he adds that by medieval standards, the devices of *amplificatio* and *digressio* were not only legitimate but

---

[21] "Literary Criticism," in *The Aims and Methods of Scholarship in Modern Languages and Literatures*, ed. James Thorpe (New York. MLA, 1968), p. 63.
[22] *Form and Meaning in Medieval Romance* (Mod. Humanities Research Assn., 1966), p. 13.

also fundamental.[23] That our idea of unity is the sole basis for assigning literary merits is obviously a questionable proposition. On the other hand, there is no reason to deny that the search for it is a legitimate critical task, provided that one does not insist on applying the same criteria in every case.

The need for this kind of critical flexibility is evident in the case of Vicente's theater as a whole and in that of the *Floresta de Enganos* in particular. It is doubtful whether this play can withstand the test of the usual critical procedure. Its unity cannot in all fairness be expected to coincide with that of, let us say, *Oedipus Rex*. But if, instead of pronouncing a hasty judgment, we are willing to view it from a different angle bearing in mind Vinaver's remarks, we may find that there are other elements which compensate for its lack of a close-knit dramatic unity.

As Waldron admirably puts it, "Vicente makes greater demands on his modern readers than most authors; the main essentials for an understanding of his work are a sense of humour and lack of critical preconceptions."[24] If the critic makes no conscientious effort to free himself of critical prejudices before undertaking to evaluate Vicente's work, he will surely do him a great disservice. Unfortunately, the students of Vicente's theater have now and then demonstrated an attitude characterized by lack of objectivity or perception.[25] It must be realized that it is faulty logic to judge the playwright in the light of what is now understood by the term "dramatist". Applying modern dramatic norms — which are after all greatly indebted to the neo-Aristotelian doctrines that

---

[23] Ibid., pp. 11-12.

[24] See the Introduction to his edition of Vicente's *Amadís de Gaula* (Manchester: Manchester Univ. Press, 1959), p. 15.

[25] Reis Brasil's case is not uncommon among critics of this field: he has channeled his energy in extolling Vicente; in a paroxysm of nationalism, he has drawn the preposterous conclusion that "Gil Vicente é o criador do teatro português; Gil Vicente é o criador do teatro peninsular; Gil Vicente é o criador do teatro moderno europeo e mundial. Todas as bases desse teatro dos nossos dias dependem da iniciação vicentina;" see the Introduction of his *Gil Vicente e o teatro moderno* (Lisbon: Minerva, 1965), p. 22. Others have committed the same error as W. C. Atkinson, namely condemning Gil Vicente for what he did not do: see his "*Comédias, tragicomédias* and *farças* in Gil Vicente," *BdF*, 11 (1950), 268-80, and also I. S. Révah's comments on Atkinson's arguments in his "La *comédia* dans l'oeuvre de Gil Vicente," *BHTP*, 2 (1951), 1-39.

became current in the Hispanic world only in the latter part of the sixteenth century [26] — to Vicente's works, and insisting on evaluating them in terms of what, in our opinion, the playwright did or did not intend to do, [27] or what we would have liked him to do rather than what he actually did, will inevitably lead us to a distorted and largely falsified idea of their functional quality.

Critics often tend to forget that Vicente wrote almost exclusively for the stage, and that his plays were generally composed on command and formed integral parts of Court festivals. Their festive quality may account to a rather large extent for the apparent heterogeneity of the elements which the playwright has blended in his art, and this in turn creates an impression of fragmentariness and dramatic incoherence in some cases.

Vicentine scholars seem inclined to agree unanimously on the lack of logic in the structure of the *Floresta de Engaños*. Count von Schack notes that

> la comedia, que lleva el raro título de *Floresta de Engaños*, es poco notable por el plan, pero superior en algunos rasgos aislados, componiendo una serie de escenas cómicas, llenas de astucia y travesura, aunque sin verdadera unidad dramática, puesto que el lazo, que las une, es sólo la semejanza del asunto y el nombre común a todas ellas. [28]

For Menéndez y Pelayo it is "una farsa *implexa*, puesto que combina dos ó tres en una, á la verdad con poco arte." [29] Aubrey Bell commented on the looseness of its structure on several occasions. [30] Wickersham Crawford considers the play "a bizarre composition" that "presents a series of deceptions and tricks with little relationship to one another." [31] William C. Atkinson calls it an "olla

---

[26] See E. C. Riley, *Cervantes's Theory of the Novel* (Oxford: Clarendon Press, 1962), Ch. i.
[27] Cf. Frye's comments on the intentional fallacy, op. cit., p. 59.
[28] *Historia de la literatura y del arte dramático en España*, trans. Eduardo de Mier (Madrid: Escritores castellanos, 1885), I, 294-95.
[29] *Antología de poetas líricos castellanos* (Madrid: Librería de Hernando, 1898), VII, ccvii.
[30] *Gil Vicente* (Oxford: Oxford Univ. Press, 1921), pp. 50, 53-54; *Portuguese Literature* (Oxford: Oxford Univ. Press, 1922), p. 119; *Estudos vicentinos*, pp. 110, 151.
[31] *Spanish Drama before Lope de Vega*, pp. 103-04.

podrida" and adds that "the critic, studying its structure, is forced to the conclusion that 'o mecanismo teatral, volvidos mais de trinta anos de experiência de representações, nada tinha adiantado'." [32] Álvaro Júlio da Costa Pimpão believes that this play "acusa... a declinação do Autor," [33] whereas T. P. Waldron refers to many of Vicente's later works —undoubtedly including the *Floresta*— as not being "strictly plays at all, but diffuse dramatic fantasies, or theatrical reviews." [34] Finally, Laurence Keates regrets that the *Floresta* is "marred by the admixture of... elements proper to the *farsa*." [35] Such verdicts are eloquent proof of the scholars' disappointment, which, consciously or unconsciously, stems from their unfulfilled desire to make this play respond to their own notions of dramatic unity.

A few of the critics just cited, as well as a good many others, have sought to account for this lack of a tightly woven structural pattern. With minor variations, their arguments center around the "primitivism" of Gil Vicente's theater in contrast to the "classicism" of the Renaissance. Some scholars contend that the non-dramatic quality of his theater should be attributed to his ignorance of the classics. [36] This implies that had he known Greek or Roman drama and the dramatic theory of antiquity, he would have oriented his craft in that direction. The validity of this assertion, however, is doubtful. True, Vicente had no direct knowledge of the classical theater. Yet, in about the middle of his career as a dramatist, he might have drawn a few lessons from Torres Naharro's *Propalladia* (Naples 1517; Seville 1520), and, later, from Sá de Miranda's Italianate play, *Os estrangeiros* (1528). That he did not adopt the modes of the neo-classical theater may suggest either that he was not interested in it, or that he was unable to

---

[32] Op. cit., pp. 274, 279; Atkinson is here quoting Óscar de Pratt, *Gil Vicente: notas e comentários* (Lisbon: Teixeira, 1931), p. 46.

[33] See the Introduction to his edition of Vicente's *Obras completas* (Barcelos: Editora do Minho, 1956), p. xlv.

[34] Op. cit., p. 14.

[35] Op. cit., pp. 124, 129.

[36] See Fidelino de Figueiredo, *Características da litteratura portuguesa* (Lisbon: Livraria Clássica, 1923), pp. 28-30, and Carolina Michaëlis, *Notas*, pp. 151 ff.

cope with its exigencies.[37] He may also have felt that neo-classical precepts would have been incompatible with his function as Court entertainer; most likely, he simply had confidence in his own artistic convictions. The fact that Vicente passed into oblivion for so long must be due primarily to his having modeled his work on medieval patterns, at a time when classical forms were so enthusiastically adopted by the rest of Europe.[38]

At any rate, we should not censure Vicente because he failed to conform to the dictates of a voice which, for one reason or other, did not appeal to him. We should rather realize that what mattered to him was not the book but rather the stage; therefore, the theatrical aspect of his plays should be the primary measure of his worth. As Gino Saviotti argues

> A teatralidade não depende só da composição geral. Pode subsistir sem a ajuda de um verdadeiro organismo narrativo, no sentido moderno, da mesma maneira que é possível encontrar-se grande pintura, maravilhosa força cromática num simples friso decorativo, ou num fragmento, que ainda não é quadro.[39]

For the sake of a better understanding of Vicente's stagecraft, we should also bear in mind that "la visión del espectador tiene otras leyes que la del crítico moroso."[40]

The lack of fairness in Vicentine criticism has been well diagnosed by Vitorino Nemésio:

> Gil Vicente teve de pagar a originalidade do seu génio. Pagou-o com uma espécie de anacronismo pessoal. Ou somos nós que, senhores de uma perspectiva literária já arrumada e nítida, em que os êxitos e os malogros se esclareçam por si, gostaríamos de vê-lo nascido um pouco

---

[37] Gino Saviotti, however, points out the case of *Inês Pereira*, in which Vicente, though unconsciously, shows that he was not incapable of coping with the new forms ("Gil Vicente poeta cómico," *BHTP*, 2, 1951, p. 202).

[38] Ibid., pp. 189-90.

[39] Ibid., p. 189. On theatricality as the essence of Gil Vicente's work, see also Albin Eduard Beau, "Gil Vicente: O aspecto 'medieval' e 'renacentista' da sua obra," in his *Estudos* (Coimbra: Acta Universitatis Conimbrigensis, 1959), I, 84, 105.

[40] Eugenio Asensio, "Las fuentes de las *Barcas* de Gil Vicente," *BHTP*, 4 (1953), 235.

mais tarde, dar tôda a medida do seu génio numa expressão mais moderna.[41]

ANALYSIS OF THE *Floresta*

With such criteria as a basis, I shall attempt an examination of the *Floresta de Enganos* in the hope of discovering any unity that may exist in its structure. I hope to show also that there exist other qualities which may enhance our vision of this particular play as well as of Gil Vicente's theater in general. The various scenes or episodes, which compose the play, will be first analyzed individually and in the order in which they occur, and their bearing on the play as a whole will then be traced.

The play opens with the entrance of a singular pair of characters, a philosopher and a simpleton, whose primary function is to acquaint the audience with the plot and introduce the first *engano*. Besides this external function, it must have been designed to incite laughter by its sharp contrast of the two extremes, wisdom and stupidity, and to ferry the audience from the real world of the Court to that of the imagination. As often in Gil Vicente's plays, this prologue is a long one and has the qualities of a play in itself.

Of all Peninsular playwrights of the early sixteenth century, Vicente makes the most varied use of the prologue.[42] Here the two personages are chained together, a fact which causes distress to the philosopher but does not produce the least feeling of discomfort in the simpleton; it is perhaps a hint that the realm of wisdom and the realm of stupidity are not as widely apart in essence as in appearance. The philosopher complains bitterly of his adverse fortune; his present misfortune has come about as punishment for his eagerness to offer his wise judgment to the services of "los muy antigos romanos," who, in his own words,

... porque la reprehensión
a todos es enojosa,
... ...

---

[41] In his *Gil Vicente: Floresta de enganos* (Lisbon: Inquérito, 1941), pp. 21-22.

[42] See Joseph A. Meredith, *Introito and Loa in the Spanish Drama of the Sixteenth Century* (Philadelphia: Univ. of Penn. Press, 1928), p. 82.

> ... me echaron en prisión,
> en cárcel muy tenebrosa.
> No bastó: mas en depués
> daquesto que oído havéis,
> ... ...
> ataron ansí comigo
> este bovo que aquí veis.   (11-20)

In addition to suffering an undeserved penalty, the philosopher repudiates the idea of being in the constant company of a fool, a humiliating and bothersome experience for a man of learning. The fool, on the other hand, appears oblivious to any notion of misfortune; instead, the only interest he expresses lies in the thought of things that would instinctively appeal to a person with a practical, rather than a speculative, turn of mind. He only cares for satisfying his bodily wants: he is presented as gluttonous and lazy:

> Dezid, nuestramo, veamos:
> ¿son mejores de comer
> las grajas o los milanos?
> Y más ¿sabéis qué yo querría?
> Dormir quatro o cinco meses.   (76-80)

In the character of the dunce are embodied the traits which typify the stupid comic personages in early Spanish drama: the dull remarks, with which he continually interrupts the philosopher's mission, his constant references to eating and sleeping, and his actual sleeping on stage. The latter, observes William S. Hendrix, "is paralleled by the philosophical theme that mankind is asleep in this world to better things."[43]

What we have here, then, is in essence a confrontation between the world of the spirit and the world of the senses. The two characters, though bound to each other, represent two widely opposite points of view which are comically accentuated in the course of the debate that comprises the entire episode. The contrast culminates when the philosopher expresses envy for the fool's lack of sensitivity:

---

[43] *Some Native Comic Types in the Early Spanish Drama*, Ohio State Univ. Contributions in Languages and Literatures, No. 1 (Columbus: Ohio State Univ. Press, 1925), p. 78.

> ¡Oh, quien no sintiesse más
> de lo malo ni de lo bueno,
> de lo suyo y de lo ageno,
> de quanto tú sentirás! (38-41)

While the *parvo* is meditating on the satisfaction of his physical needs, the philosopher continues to paint his affliction. His fortune has led him ironically from Scylla to Charybdis. For fear of finding a stupid wife he decided never to marry, but now, he finds himself in an even worse situation. Though spared a stupid wife, he is married, in a sense, to the fool:

> Que lo traiga desta suerte
> al comer y al cenar,
> al dormir y platicar;
> esto so pena de muerte
> que no lo pueda dexar
> hasta el morir. (21-26)

The figure of the philosopher is basically full of pathos. But the playwright has admirably combined his pathos with the simpleton's tendencies in a highly comic scene; he has not failed to exploit every possibility of adding humor to it, such as situation, characterization and the incoherent quality of the dialogue. Even though most of the time the two characters talk of different things, they appear to debate the same issue.

At last, as soon as the fool falls asleep, the philosopher has the opportunity to carry out his mission, namely to introduce "una fiesta de alegría," and give a summary of its plot in prose "por ir más declarado." Before withdrawing from the stage, he also introduces the merchant of the first episode who "pensando d'engañar, / ha de quedar engañado." [44] Our play then is introduced from the outset as a *fiesta de alegría*, something, that is, which is to cause mirth and delight the audience. This, along with the overtones of the introductory scene, reveals the spirit of the playwright's entire undertaking.

---

[44] Ronald B. Williams has indicated (op. cit., p. 47), with reference to this play, that "a single scene represents a succession of places," and that "transition is indicated by means of an empty stage, and by statements of characters relative to place."

The proverb "si queréis matar al cuerdo, / atalde un necio al pie" (44-45)[45] may have served as the point of departure for the development of the prologue. Vicente's fondness for folk materials is well known. His exploitation of popular wisdom is best illustrated in *Inês Pereira* (1523), where the proverb "Mais quero asno que me leve que cavalo que me derrube" is at the core of the play — though the myth of the play's composition around this proverb as a test of Vicente's dramatic capabilities is no longer generally accepted.[46]

With the opening of the following picaresque episode, we are transported into a world of fraud and deception which will assert itself repeatedly throughout the play. The pattern on which the theme of deceit unfolds follows faithfully the popular belief that "el que engaña, engañado se halla."[47] In this case, deceit is inextricably associated with money. No sooner has the merchant appeared on stage than he engages in a eulogy of money and the omnipotence traditionally ascribed to it:

> Determíno de fazer
> minhas casas muito bem,
> porque quem dinheiro tem
> fará tudo o que quiser.   (141-144)

Knowing, however, that he is already doomed to fall victim to his own deceitful designs, we can immediately sense the irony of his statement. These few words of his also suffice to paint a vivid portrait of his character.

His self-confidence —acquired through a long experience of exploiting needy people— blinds him: while his prospective prey describes her wretchedness in the gloomiest possible terms, he does not have the slightest suspicion that under the disguise of a widow

---

[45] Cf. Gonzalo Correas, *Vocabulario de refranes y frases proverbiales* (Madrid, 1924), p. 459: "Si quieres matar a un cuerdo, átale al pie un necio."
[46] See I. S. Révah's Introduction to his edition of *Inês Pereira*, BHTP, 4 (1953), 77.
[47] Correas, *Vocabulario*, p. 179. For analogous folk motifs, see Stith Thompson, *Motif-Index of Folk-Literature*, FF Communications, Nos. 106-09, 116-17 (Helsinki: Academia Scientiarum Fennica, 1932-1936), K1600-1699 (Deceiver falls into own trap), and John E. Keller, *Motif-Index of Mediaeval Spanish Exempla* (Knoxville: Univ. of Tenn. Press, 1959), J1510 (The cheater cheated).

hides a poor squire determined to defraud "um ladrão." This is a kind of play within a play, since, in their effort to dupe each other, both merchant and squire conceal their true selves and act as if they were impersonating other people. The crafty merchant professes to be moved by pity upon hearing of the widow's plight, and takes pains to show that he makes a personal sacrifice before buying her forged bill: "ora, em fim, quero ser tolo sandeu, / e só por vos socorrer" (219-220). The bargain concluded and the widow gone, the merchant tells himself how fortunate he has been in that she was a rather easy prey or, perhaps, he seeks an excuse for his action: "nam-na esfolara eu / s'ela doutra casta fôra" (245-246). Yet his satisfaction over the very favorable termination of the bargain will not last; the widow's servant-girl will soon return to dispel his illusions:

> Mercador, quereis saber?
> Bem enganado ficastes,
> que a viúva que enganastes
> era homem, e não molher.
> E mais, é vento
> êsse seu conhecimento;
> êle o assinou e nam mais.
> Assi que os dez mil reais
> leixai-os no testamento.   (247-255)

Had the scene ended with these words of the *môça*, it would have been, dramatically, far more appropriate; but the deceived merchant remains on stage to introduce the next episode. One might expect him to react to the bad news, but he does not. His self-critical comment ("crede que quem fôr tirano, / tem seu dinheiro perdido" — 256-257) is by no means the reaction of the usurer who has just been swindled of his money. He who speaks here is the actor who has now assumed the role of an objective commentator. So detached is he from his previous role that he can make moral reflections. Thus the barrier which separated play from reality is broken at this point.

Equally unexpected are the last words of the impostor, as he leaves the merchant's upon the conclusion of the fraudulent transaction:

> Nam havia em Portugal,
> nos tempos mais ancianos,

> tantas maneiras d'enganos,
> nem tantos males dum mal.   (238-241)

No matter how much truth this outburst may contain, the fact that it comes from the lips of one who has just deceived renders it highly comic.

Practically everything in this episode contributes to the establishment of the overall comic structure; the interdependence of character and situation is explicit in the deceitful contest between the money-loving merchant and the needy "widow". Though the usurer has conventionally served as a butt for satire, the manner in which he is treated here is peculiarly Vicentine. He is presented as so self-confident that he cannot, even for a moment, perceive that he is being fooled as to the very identity of his opponent. Disguise is an additional device responsible to a great extent for the general comic atmosphere. So are the asides of the shrewd, outspoken servant-girl.

In the character of the merchant, the playwright is also satirizing an abuse which was not uncommon in his days, that of usury. It seems, however, that his intentions do not go beyond the borderline of humor; he is seeking neither to instruct nor to reform, but is simply interested in the subject as another means of inciting laughter.

The transition to the following episode is made less abrupt by the mention, in the course of the fraudulent bargain, of King Telebaño, in whose kingdom the action of the entire play is to unfold. We are more or less warned by this deception as to what we should subsequently expect. Indeed, as we are soon to see, deceit is rampant in Telebaño's kingdom.

The world of esthetic reality of the first deceit fades in the background as that of fantasy comes now into focus. The merchant is succeeded on the stage by Cupid, whose expression of pain —amorous this time— echoes those of the philosopher in the prologue and of the feigned widow. The love-stricken Cupid's long lament and the description of his failure to attain the object of his love are profoundly ironic, for one would hardly expect to see Cupid wounded by his own arrows:

> ¿A quién contaré mis quexas,
> a quién diré mi tormento?

>   ¿Remedio, por qué te alexas
>   de ver Amor que solo dexas
>   neste término momento?   (266-270)

Equally ironic is his claim:

>   Los que me pintan ciego,
>   no es ansí como conviene;
>   que Amor tantos ojos tiene
>   como de muertes me ruego.   (276-279)

Erwin Panofsky tells us that as a result of the tendency to interpret allegorically his physical aspects —a tendency first noted in Roman poetry— virtually all representations of Cupid in art and literature, after "Mythographus III", would have him blind or blindfolded. As blindness was associated with evil, blind Cupid came to be conceived as a *diavolo*. So precise a significance had his blindness in the fourteenth century, that "his image could be changed from a personification of Divine Love to a personification of illicit Sensuality, and vice versa, by simply adding, or removing, the bandage;" this duality was expressed, in the Renaissance, in the conflict between *amor sacro* and *amor profano*.[48] Vicente seems to conceive his subject in secular rather than in religious terms; by "removing the bandage," he does not suggest that he eliminates the element of sensuality from Cupid's intentions; he simply renders his caricature of the god more complete: even though Cupid can see perfectly well — otherwise he could hardly be a serious suitor —, he still inflicts upon himself what he was conventionally thought to inflict upon others. The bandage is missing but Cupid behaves as if he still retained it.

Cupid's diction throughout the episode shows him to be a courtly lover; all the fundamental conceits of the courtly code are present: the beloved, Grata Celia, is addressed as "flor del más florido huerto!" (282). Besides being the lover's *señora*, she is described as indifferent to his attentions, as cruel and ungrateful, and, what is more, as taking pleasure at his suffering: "... bien sé el mal que me quieres, / y los gozos y plazeres / que recibes con

---

[48] See "Blind Cupid," in his *Studies in Iconology* (New York: Oxford Univ. Press, 1939), pp. 95-128.

mis llagas" (298-300). Furthermore, love is referred to as all-consumming fire, as torment, and as death: "Oh ingrata pecador, / rasga el coraçón esquivo, / que mataste al dios d'amor" (291-293).

A strange world, indeed, has opened before our eyes; a world composed mainly of pagan mythology and a strong dose of courtly matter. Gil Vicente has made an extensive use of courtly love in his theater, although, as T. R. Hart has noted, its use "varies strikingly from play to play."[49] In the present case, its use obeys the playwright's desire to control the flight of imagination and bring the action from the purely fantastic plane down closer to that of verifiable reality. Vicente, in other words, has not allowed himself to establish a wholly supernatural world merely for its own sake. What he undoubtedly has sought to do is to maintain and enrich the initially established atmosphere of comedy, to carry out his plan of providing a *fiesta de alegría*. To this end, he has made Cupid a comic personage by caricaturing him in a variety of ways: he has humanized him, subjecting him to the pains of love, which, ironically, he normally administers himself. What is more, he has transformed him from God of Love to a courtly lover. Finally, he has made him fail in his amorous pursuit, deceived by the very object of his desire.

Unable otherwise, owing to his *reductio ad humanum*, to overcome the obstacles which hinder the conquest of his desired goal, the most important of which is, needless to mention, Grata Celia's resistance, Cupid decides to resort to deception:

> Cúmpleme de usar engaño,
> que el engaño no es estraño;
> antes se usa cada hora,
> y la verdad d'año en año.   (312-315)

His first victim is Apollo himself, whom he first reassures that he is not in love and then persuades that his temple will soon be devastated along with King Telebano's city; and that at the cause of all this is Telebano's daughter, Grata Celia, whom Cupid calumniates as having secretly wrought many evils offensive to the goddesses. Cupid's tale reaches its climax when he makes

---

[49] In "Courtly Love in *Don Duardos*," *RomN*, 2 (1961), 103.

Apollo believe that the only remedy which can prevent the oncoming disaster lies in the latter's ability to convince King Telebano that he should

> [Llevar] su hija daquí
> a aquella serra Minea,
> adonde sin ella se vea,
> y haga penitencia allí
> por que perdonada sea. (345-349)
> . . . .
> Y Grata Celia escondida,
> allí sola, desterrada,
> salvará también su vida;
> pues que siendo oferecida,
> será libre y perdonada. (355-359)

Cupid is naturally aware of his delinquent behavior but he wishes to believe that so long as he succeeds in conquering Grata Celia, the means he employs are justified:

> Yo bien sé que erro ahora,
> mas es por sanar un daño.
> Perdóname, mi señora,
> que el mundo triste dagora
> se llama templo d'engaño. (375-379)

In fact this first *engano* of his will have the effect of a chain reaction, as deceit follows deceit throughout the rest of the play. A similar pattern of development will be followed later in Tirso's *El burlador de Sevilla*.[50] It seems hardly necessary to add that Cupid is in fact a Don Juan though in an embryonic stage. The symptoms of the behavior of both are by and large the same. Selfish pleasure is the motive and the object of their deceptions; both have a warped sense of moral values; like Don Juan, Cupid is the epitome of a corrupt world in which deceit is used "cada hora, / y la verdad d'año en año."

In the figure of Apollo, pagan mythology is blended with Christian dogma. When King Telebano appears at his temple to pray, Apollo gives him the kind of advice one would expect

---

[50] For which see Bruce Wardropper, "*El burlador de Sevilla*: a Tragedy of Errors," *PQ*, 36 (1957), 61-71.

from an ecclesiastic rather than a pagan god (we are reminded of a similar situation in Alfonso de Valdés' *Diálogo de Mercurio y Carón*, where the preaching is assigned to Mercurio):

>   Vuestra Alteza reze breve
>   y obre obras de sancto,
>   que el rezar no monta tanto
>   como hazer lo que se deve.
>   El rezar es como flores
>   y flores las oraciones,
>   y el fructo, dizen doctores,
>   las obras son los amores,
>   y no las buenas razones.   (385-393)

This distinction between works and words, between reality and appearance, is sound Christian doctrine and it occurs elsewhere in Gil Vicente.[51] To have, however, a figure from pagan mythology make use of Christian precepts and preach on the proper kind of Christian conduct, is not only peculiar but deliberately comic: it is in accordance with Vicente's general scheme in this play, of producing comic effects by having the wrong character pronounce the right judgment. We have already seen examples of this technique in the cases of the disguised squire and of Cupid. Celestina's fondness for moral *sententiae* is a well-known precedent.

To exploit further the possibilities for comedy which his presentation of Apollo offers, Mestre Gil makes him an expert in feminine psychology: informing King Telebano that a member of his household has provoked the implacable wrath of the goddesses Verecinta, Juno, and Pallas, he takes advantage of the opportunity to explain the working of the feminine mind:

>   Son diesas muy furiosas:
>   ya sabéis que las mugeres,
>   quando están más amorosas,
>   más blandas, más piadosas,
>   no son menos que crueles;
>   ¿qué harán siendo sañosas?   (420-425)

---

[51] Cf., for example, the *Triunfo do inverno*, fo. 179 c, and the *Tragicomédia de Amadis de Gaula*, fo. 138 d.

Apollo's ultimatum marks the beginning of dramatic conflict. King Telebano is confronted with the dilemma which constitutes a *topos* in literature, sacred as well as profane (cf. the Old Testament story of Abraham's sacrifice of Isaac, which is alluded to by Gil Vicente himself in lines 759-760, and Agamemnon's sacrifice of Iphigenia in Euripides' *Iphigenia at Aulis*). Despite the obvious similarity in situation between the two, the Biblical and Vicente's story, there is a substantial difference: whereas for Telebano there are alternatives between which he must choose — namely, the destruction of his city or the loss of his daughter —, for Abraham the issue is not one of real choice. He can choose only between obedience and disobedience; his strong commitment to God, however, automatically rules out the second alternative. Moreover, though neither Telebano nor Abraham questions the justness of the command, Telebano chooses very easily for one who is presented with a choice. Yet, for a father who suddenly realizes that he is about to lose his daughter, there is nothing more natural than intolerable pain and lament:

>¡Oh graves angustias mías,
>lágrimas dell ánima mía!
>¡Oh hija de mi alegría!
>¿Qué tales serán mis días
>fuera de tu compañía?
>Quedarás en las montañas,
>naquella Minea sierra,
>y mis beços y mis canas
>mucho en breve serán tierra.   (444-452)

His daughter's appearance and her inquiries as to what has so changed his aspect intensify Telebano's agony, the more so because he cannot disclose to her the cause of it. Instead, he must lead her to her destiny by deceit; he therefore asks her to go on a hunting trip with him, pretending that this will suffice to lessen his grief. He entrusts the administration of his kingdom, during his absence, to the Chief Justice, whom he considers impeccably educated and consistently *cuerdo*; in fact, in addressing him, the king makes use of the same epithets, *sabio y prudente*, that Grata Celia had used when referring to her father: this accentuates the good impression he has of his Chief Justice. The playwright has made it highly ironic, however, for subsequent events disprove the king's good opinion of the Justice. The administrative matter arranged, Telebano and his daughter are on their way to the sham hunt which will *perhaps* (note the intentional change in certainty now) restore him to good humor. Though ignorant of the entire issue, Grata Celia notices with wondering surprise that the farther they go the more apprehensive she becomes.

The playwright demands that we let the king and his daughter go on their way while we stay to witness a new farcical incident. It involves none other than Telebano's temporary replacement, the Chief Justice, and it is an extremely comic elaboration of the motif of the disastrous effect of love on an aged person, of which there are antecedents in Vicente's theater (cf. *O velho da horta*, the *Comédia de Rubena*, and *O triunfo do inverno*). Once again, there is a brusque change of tone: we are made to descend, in a sense, from the level of the sublime to that of the ridiculous. Strangely enough, this scene, which is undeniably the most delightfully funny of the entire play, is omitted in the summary of the plot. For Aubrey Bell, this is an indication that the *Floresta* is made up of parts composed at different periods of Vicente's dramatic career.[52] Nevertheless, this particular episode is not as independent as it might appear at first sight: in addition to the fact that it revolves around the same basic note, that of deceit, it is related to the mythological story by virtue of its protagonist, whom King Telebano has personally appointed as his temporary successor in the administration of his kingdom. What takes place in this kingdom, during the king's absence, may serve as an implicit commentary on the king's decision to make this appointment; in effect, this episode proves that Telebano has been fooled in his high esteem for, and confidence in, the integrity and discretion of his Chief Justice. It may be argued, moreover, that this scene counterbalances the emotional effects produced by Telebano's situation, though, at the same time, it creates suspense in the anticipation of its outcome. It also serves to re-enforce the impression of a kingdom dominated by deceit, which was first established in the episode of the usurious merchant; not only the subjects but also the administrators are corrupt. Finally, from a

---

[52] See his *Gil Vicente*, p. 54, as well as his *Estudos vicentinos*, pp. 77, 151.

technical point of view, this scene creates the illusion of the duration of Telebano's trip to the mountain.

As the scene opens, the Chief Justice is shown in his study reading in a law book. He is caricatured right from the start: being a jurist, he is supposed to know correct Latin; yet the first words he utters are in macarronic Latin. The refusal of the young girl, who comes to ask for advice on some legal matter, to enter despite his insistence ("Estais agora estudando / só, e eu sam grande já" — 502-503), suggests the moral reputation the learned justice enjoys, which apparently is not compatible with King Telebano's high opinion of him. When the girl remarks: "Sabeis quê, senhor Doctor? / Vós pareceis-me travêsso" (513-514), he hastens to respond that he is not to be feared for he is well advanced in age, which, in view of the convention already referred to, confirms that her suspicions are not groundless. She does not trust the way he looks at her, and with reason. His insistence that she enter and her repeated refusals animate the dialogue and accelerate the tempo of the action. Unsuccessful in his effort to weaken her resistance by any other means, the impassioned justice begins to entreat her in a courtly fashion!:

> ¡Oh, entrad acá, señora,
> mi sagrado paraíso! (522-523)

> ...¿qué haré yo, mis flores,
> a los ojos matadores
> que me cegaron los míos? (528-530)

> ¡Oh mi perla preciosa!
> No me hagáis entender
> que sin vos haya hermosa. (534-536)

This set of perfectly conventional conceits leaves no room for doubt as to his ulterior motives. The playwright has once more availed himself of this chance to employ the courtly tradition as an instrument of character delineation; he makes the justice ridiculous by having him present himself as a courtly lover. Noteworthy is the girl's realistic reaction:

> Quem tal quer
> nam havia de ter molher,
> e fermosa como a vossa. (531-533)

Under the overwhelming impact of passion, the justice has become unmindful of his age, his marital status and the responsibilities of his position. In his eagerness to strike an agreement with the girl, he will not hesitate to sacrifice even his professional integrity:

> Yo no quiero
> de vos plata ni dinero,
> mas privar con vos por cierto
> en lugar mucho secreto,
> por deziros quánto os quiero.
>   Yo daré, juro a Dios,
> la sentencia en vuesso hecho;
> y aunque no tengáis derecho
> todo ello saldrá por vos,
> y haréis vuesso provecho.   (541-550)

Under these circumstances, and being as astute as she is, the girl pretends to give in and asks him to visit her secretly at night. The justice is too overcome by the prospect of reward to grasp the irony of her words, when she asks with affected innocence: "assoviaes vós bem, meu rei?" (557). His whole attitude makes him an appropriate victim of the pranks that the girl engineers at his expense:

> Oh, como hei d'enganar
> um doutor que se enganou!
>   Alguidar, ora vem cá,
> e faremos o formento;
> que negro contentamento
> o negro doutor terá,
> do que lh'há de sair vento.   (563-569)

Her song also foretells, in a more emphatic way, his eventual disillusionment.

Still forgetting that he is not fit for the type of role he has chosen to perform, the justice appears at the girl's door, following her instructions with utmost care. Once inside, he becomes the butt of her constant shafts of ridicule. She dominates him and the entire scene, now with her spontaneous wit, now with well calculated mischievous tricks. Time and again her caustic remarks contradict, point by point, the king's judgment of him (e.g. "Crede que mao é d'achar / um letrado ser discreto"—575-576). The hilariousness of the situation is greatly enhanced by her having him undergo humiliation after humiliation. He, nevertheless, complies, without a trace of objection, with her demands that he whisper, take care not to cough, replace his garments with those of a baker-woman, and finally, that he sift flour. She even offers him a sifting lesson for she is not pleased with his work. During all this ritual, she is careful to rekindle, from time to time, his hopes of attaining the object of his desire. It is the entertainment of such illusions that matters to the justice; as he confesses, it is all for the sake of love:

> Paciencia;
> porque juro en mi conciencia
> que este texto yo no lo entiendo.
> Peró si yo estoy cirniendo,
> es en loor y reverencia
> del amor a que me riendo.
>   Estas bueltas no sé yo.
> *Dulcis amor, qui me vis?*
> Que no se aprende en París
> este lavor en que estó.
> ¡Oh amor!   (617-627)

His lack of perception, caused by his infatuation which, in turn, is not completely unrelated to his bookish nature, is what renders his pathos ludicrous. His own world is quite incompatible with the world into which his new role has led him, something he failed to realize before stepping out of his study. Furthermore, he is not receptive to any hint at all; otherwise he would have noticed the relevance of the girl's aphorism, even if it is stated in a different context: "em tudo o que fazemos / há mister manhas assaz / segundo o mundo que temos" (610-612).

The scene reaches its climax when the justice becomes the laughing stock of the *velha*, who mistakes him, initially, for a negro baker-woman and subsequently showers him with epithets which would not normally be encountered in his books. When at last his real identity is revealed to her, she ridicules him, aided by the girl, with such violence that he has to flee as hastily as he can. He will return only to claim his garments, but in this, too, he will be rebuffed. It is still inconceivable to him "que una rapaza de un año / hiziera tan grande engaño / a un doctor hecho en Sena" (738-740); and he resolves to reenter his world and resume his duties (oddly enough, this is the first time that he shows concern for his reputation):

>   Será más sano
>   callar hecho tan profano
>   y olvidar esta guerra,
>   y irme a juzgar la tierra.   (741-744)

King Telebano then has not only been deceived by his superior, Apollo, but also by his inferior, the justice, who has failed to obey his instructions and to prove worthy of his trust.

All three characters who appear in this scene are superbly drawn; their every word and movement succeeds in creating an extraordinarily fast farcical rhythm. The playwright's masterly handling of contrasting levels of speech merits special attention: he has harmonized the flowery diction of the justice with the speech, full of mockery, of the *môça*, and the crude and eventually harsh, though in some cases Latinized with humoristic intent, terminology of the *velha* — which reminds us of the Latin proverb in the mouth of the *forneira* in the *Triunfo do inverno* (fo. 182 c). Equally noticeable, from a comic point of view, is of course the justice's attempt to imitate Negro speech.

Beyond this, laughter is also a matter of inappropriateness: in order to enrich the comic tone, Vicente has sought again, and quite effectively, the aid of his favorite technique of occasionally making his characters say and do things which would not normally be expected of them. Most conspicuous for not adhering to any sense of decorum is, apart from the justice's, the case of the *velha* who cites famous jurists and uses Latin expressions:

>   Dizede, Doutor da má-hora,
>   e falai-me per latim:
>   que diz o Bártolo aqui?   (674-676)

>   No Baldo acharíeis, Doutor,
>   essa negra amassadura
>   ou na sagrada Escretura?   (693-695)

>   E moça queríeis vós?
>   E *per quam regula*, micer,

cuidou vosso parecer
que já a tínheis nas piós?   (702-705)

Another example of this kind of parodic intention of speech is the *frade*'s *sermon joyeux* at the beginning of the *Auto de Mofina Mendes*, which is full of famous names jumbled in the context.[53]

It is the *velha* also who summarizes the justice's vain ambitions: "Que má-hora cá tornastes, / que tam tarde começastes / a ser doutor e pàdeira" (690-692).

We ought at this point to note that Gil Vicente's satire, like that of fifteenth-century and earlier Peninsular writers[54] and of the seventeenth-century *comedia*,[55] is not political but ethical; it is individuals rather than the institutions themselves which are corrupt. In his caricature of Telebano's Chief Justice, in other words, Vicente does not seek to degrade Justice in general; he simply exposes the abuses of a particular individual. He loses no opportunity to show his repugnance for people who either do what they are not supposed to do, or who do not know what to do. The shipwreck, in the *Triunfo do inverno*, is caused by the seamen's ignorance and inability to carry out their duties; they have accepted responsibility for the ship but they do not take their responsibility seriously. And then, there is the figure of Justice, in the *Frágoa de amor* (fos. 154v-155r), hunchbacked and with crooked staff and broken scales— epitomizing the aberrations of individual justices— who asks to be refashioned in the forge before the arrival of the Queen. For Vicente, then, it is not the established social structure that needs to be corrected but the deviations from it.

With Telebano and Grata Celia's arrival at the sierra Minea, we must once again resume our interrupted flight into the world of fantasy, a world not essentially different from that of the foolish old justice, since it, too, is filled with fraud and deception. Cupid's case is identical with that of the Chief Justice, in the sense that he, too, has gone through so much trouble only to see

---

[53] Fos. 20v-21r. For this sermon, see I. S. Révah, *Les sermons de Gil Vicente* (Lisbon, 1949).

[54] For which see Pierre LeGentil, *La poésie lyrique espagnole et portugaise a la fin du Moyen Age*, I (Rennes: Plihon, 1949), 407-20.

[55] Cf., for example. Lope's Comendadores.

his hopes thwarted. Therefore, and from the same perspective, the episode involving the justice can be said to prefigure Cupid's ultimate rebuff. Awaiting the fruition of his fraudulent plan, Cupid still wears the garb of the courtly lover.

Upon their arrival at the mountain, King Telebano reveals the truth to his daughter and asks to be pardoned for having deceived her against his own will. The unwelcome news fills her with utmost despair:

> ¡Oh triste yo!
> Ya sé quién esto ordenó:
> Copido hizo estos daños.
> Oh mis tristes quinze años,
> mal haya quien los mató.   (761-765)
>
> Saquéisme, padre, la vida
> de que fuistes causador.   (771-772)
>
> Perded manzilla de mí
> y matadme, señor padre.   (775-776)

In an effort to console her, Telebano assures her that this is where she will encounter her greatest fortune. No sooner has he departed than Cupid appears to declare his love in courtly rhetoric. In effect, the entire scene between these two characters seems to be an exercise in *dulce retórica*. Unlike the preceding episodes, the movement of the action is slowed down as the general tone becomes loftier. This portion of the mythological scene is rather like an extended *serranilla*: Cupid in his courtship of Grata Celia goes basically through the same stages as the lover of such a poem. He is as confident as the merchant was that his reward is near and in accordance with his wishes: "bendito seas engaño / que con tu poder estraño, / todo acabas quanto quieres" (796-798). He wastes no time in pressing his love in melifluous terms:

> Prefeción de las mugeres,
> vos me quitastes la vida
> y la tenéis consumida,
> y mis bienes y plazeres.
> Y viéndoos puesta
> en esta brava floresta
> y entre estas espessuras,

> dexé el cielo a escuras
> por ver la claridá vuestra.   (804-812)

Whereas Cupid is wholly absorbed by his highly emotional rhetoric, Grata Celia's mental faculties function perfectly well: when he demands the reward for having served her, she retorts quite logically: "pues vos sois el dios Copido, / que todo amor tiene en sí, / ¿qué amor pedís a mí?" (849-851). Cupid has apparently underestimated her; not only does she refuse to yield to his requests, but she even manages, by means of deception, to reverse the situation and have him chain himself in her place. Once free, she points out the falsity of his love, since true love never deceives, and states categorically: "no quiero escuchar amores, / pues nunca los conocí" (900-901). She proceeds to denounce men and the women who trust them:

> Bendita sea la muger
> que de los hombres no fía,
> y maldita la que confía
> en su dañoso querer;
> y bendita
> toda muger que se quita
> de oír sus dulces engaños.   (902-908)
>
> Como río furioso
> son los hombres, sin descanso;
> porque adó corre más manso,
> allí está más peligroso,
> porque es hondo aquel remanso.   (911-915)

Cupid is made to realize the futility of his elaborate scheme; he blames the overpowering effect of love (the *amor vincit omnia* motif), and delivers an equally caustic tirade against womankind:

> ¡Oh mugeres, oh mugeres!
> Robadoras de las vidas,
> crueles, desconocidas,
> destruición de plazeres.
> Coriosas,
> ufanas, desamorosas,
> autorizadas, movibles,
> y de todo envejosas,
> que tienen cosas terribles.   (931-939)

The interplay of deceits is to continue, however, for Cupid has not yet learned his lesson. He will make use of deceit at the expense of a rustic to set himself free. But the playwright will provide a climactically ironic end to the action, by having the master-deceiver victimized a second time by Grata Celia, for the conquest of whom he has given rise to so much confusion. He will even be made to refute what he said earlier against women, saying now:

> las mugeres a una mano
> ser la prefeción del mundo,
> en la tierra el soberano,
> en el cielo el bien segundo.   (1053-1056)

To no avail, however. It is obvious that whereas for Grata Celia the mountain has been a kind of Purgatory, from which she will finally be saved, for Cupid it has been a symbol of extreme humiliation and endless adversity.

The comic incident of the shepherd whom Cupid tricks into chaining himself is highly effective, from a theatrical point of view. The shepherd feels he is in love but he does not know with whom, which may imply that he is in love simply with the idea of being in love — like Don Rosvel, in the *Comédia do viúvo*, who loves both Paula and Melicia but cannot choose between the two. [56] He can only guess by the strength of his feelings that his beloved must be "a mor senhora / que se criou em Veneza" (981-982). But, unlike Cupid or the Chief Justice, he is fully aware of his place in society: he understands that it is ridiculous for him to be in love especially if his beloved is of such extraordinary beauty:

> Em mi tal amor que monta?   (1000)
>
> Que presta a um vilam roim
> ir amar tam alta estrêla?
> Eu sam indino pastor,
> pobre, vestido de pele.   (1007-1010)

His case contradicts the stilnovist concept, according to which *al cor gentil ripara sempre amore*: he is quite capable of feeling love,

---

[56] See T. R. Hart's Introduction to his edition of Vicente's *Obras dramáticas castellanas* (Madrid: Espasa-Calpe, 1962), p. xxxix.

though not perhaps to the same degree that a courtier would, but he realizes that his social position makes it impossible for his love to be returned.

This incident functions, by contrast, as a commentary on Cupid's general attitude. It is, at the same time, Vicente's *coup de grâce* against the precepts of the courtly code: for although the shepherd feels the pangs of love, he still thinks of his cows; furthermore, in his speech he mingles courtly with rustic imagery:

> Um fraco pastor matais
> e nam é cousa honesta;
> que a cárrega que lançais
> à mula que carregais
> pesa muito mais que a bêsta.   (1015-1019)

With Cupid still in chains, the play is brought to an end in a manner not unfamiliar to the reader of Vicente's theater: through the intervention of a sort of *deus ex machina*, Ventura, Grata Celia is united in marriage with the Prince of Greece, who happens to come wandering by with his entourage over the mountain. Nothing in the course of the action leads to such a denouement. In a way, it is comparable to the happy end of the *Comédia do viúvo*, where the situation is saved by the intervention of an off-stage spectator, King John himself —who performs a function quite similar to that of Ventura in this play as he decides that Don Rosvel should marry Paula— and of Don Rosvel's brother, Don Gilberto, who helps to solve the problem of finding a husband for Melicia. All that happens in this episode is the effect of Cupid's deceitful motives; Grata Celia tricks him twice but only in self-defense. Though hardly convincing, the final marriage may symbolize the "stability of the social order under the sanction of divine law," as customary in the Spanish plays of the Golden Age.[57]

Ventura's role is a curious blend of go-between and Divine Providence. Most often referred to as Fortuna —though the name Ventura threatened to prevail at one time— she is among the few members of the classical pantheon that remained alive following the decline and fall of ancient Rome, as is shown by the wealth of

---

[57] A. A. Parker, "The Approach to the Spanish Drama of the Golden Age." *TDR*, 4 (1959), 49.

allusions to her both in medieval and Renaissance literature. She survived into the Christian era because she represented an idea which was as indispensable to the Christian mind as to the pagan.[58] And "while... the pagan idea managed to keep a fairly large number of devotees, a compromise with Christianity was effected for others, and a genuinely Christian figure was created, retaining the title and the apparatus of the pagan cult."[59] Ventura, in this play, seems to be in the service of the Christian God, though she preserves certain characteristics of the older cults, namely her functions as Fortuna Dux and Fortune of Love:

> Pongo figura:
> dize qualquier criatura—
> esto bien lo sabéis vos—
> "quizo Dios y la Ventura."
> Primero se nombra Dios,
> porque es cosa más segura.
>   Yo os guío por acá,
> por muy venturosa vía,
> por dar nueva alegría
> a la reina que aquí está.
> De manera
> que ella es principal heredera
> en la gran Persia Mayor,
> y vos, muy alto señor,
> no la neguéis de pracera.   (1180-1194)

This mythological episode is the longest in the play and the most intricately wrought. The characters are inextricably enmeshed in a situation sustained mainly through a series of deceits which are causally related to one another. Though basically a romantic story, it is satirical in intention. This is evident in the contrasting nature of the protagonists; Cupid's tireless efforts to attain the favors of his beloved are ridiculously frustrated by Grata Celia's lack of a romantic disposition. There are moments of genuine dramatic intensity, in King Telebano's case, but they are of very short duration and do not in any way destroy the overtones of comedy and burlesque, to which practically everything has been

---

[58] See Howard R. Patch, *The Goddess Fortuna in Mediaeval Literature* (Cambridge, Mass.: Harvard Univ. Press, 1927), esp. pp. 3-4, 14-15, 39.
[59] Ibid., p. 34.

subordinated. Besides, Telebano's affliction is essentially the ultimate result of his ignorance of Cupid's plotting. The second half of the episode constitutes a battle of the sexes, as Cupid and Grata Celia exchange diatribes against each other's sex. In this, too, Cupid is the loser.

An eloquent testimony to the fact that virtually everything has served as a pretext for burlesque is Vicente's treatment of the pagan deities. Apollo and Cupid are stripped of their original attributes and are brought down to earth. What is more, they are made fun of, Apollo by being tricked into becoming an accomplice to Cupid's designs, and, subsequently, by giving a false oracle to Telebano. Cupid is made the constant target of Vicente's satirical shafts. Ventura, though also personified, does not lend herself to comic treatment since, as already mentioned, she still held a respectable place in the medieval mentality by having reconciled herself with Christian dogma.

The element which has most conspicuously suffered Vicente's attack is the courtly love tradition, as reflected in Cupid's pose and linguistic preciosity, which are both made to produce negative results — neutralized by Grata Celia's lack of receptiveness on the one hand, and by the shepherd's admixture of courtly and rustic diction, on the other.

It is in this episode also that the double meaning of the play's title is best revealed. *Floresta* signifies "den Schauplatz der vom Menschen unberührten Wildnis," on the one hand, and "die Eigenart des menschlichen Lebens in der Welt," on the other.[60] The notion of the forest as a reflection of the world, to which the Duke's words point ("Muchas cosas de no crer / hallo por esta floresta" — 1087-1088),[61] has well-known antecedents. The forest held a certain amount of dread, for the medieval man, and was therefore looked upon with an unfavorable eye.[62] It is precisely the metaphor of the dark forest that Dante employs to express more forcefully his despair about the depravity of the world, or life, in the opening lines of the *Inferno*:

---

[60] Rainer Hess, "Die Naturauffassung Gil Vicentes," in *Aufsätze zur Portugiesischen Kulturgeschichte*, 5 (1965), 6.

[61] Ibid., p. 5.

[62] See John Ruskin, *Modern Painters* (Boston: Dana Estes, 1856?), III, 272-73.

> Nel mezzo del cammin di nostra vita
> mi ritrovai per una *selva oscura*
> che la diritta via era smarrita.
> Ah quanto a dir qual era è cosa dura
> esta selva selvaggia e aspra e forte,
> che nel pensier rinnova la paura!   (I, 1-6) [63]

The same analogy, forest-world, becomes more explicit in his *Convivio*:

> L'adolescente, che entra ne *la selva erronea di questa vita*, non saprebbe tenere lo buono cammino, se da li suoi maggiori no li fosse mostrato. [64]

Similarly, before Dante, Rabanus Maurus held that "silva est mundus iste." [65]

Vicente's vision of this world is identical, as his repeated allusions to its deceitfulness show:

> Nam havia em Portugal,
> nos tempos mais ancianos,
> tantas maneiras d'enganos,
> nem tantos males dum mal.   (238-241)
>
> ... el engaño no es estraño;
> antes se usa cada hora,
> y la verdad d'año en año.   (313-315)
>
> ... el mundo triste dagora
> se llama templo d'engaño.   (378-379)
>
> ... em tudo o que fazemos
> há mister manhas assaz
> segundo o mundo que temos.   (610-612)
>
> ¡Oh, quántos modos d'engaños
> ha hí en esta triste vida!   (924-925)

He makes similar reflections in the *Auto da festa*. [66]

---

[63] I quote from Natalino Sapegno's edition of the *Divina Commedia* (Florence: Nuova Italia, 1960). The italics, here and in the following quotation, are mine.

[64] IV, xxiv, 12. The reference is to G. Busnelli and G. Vandelli's edition (Florence: Felice le Monnier, 1964).

[65] *Allegoriae in Sacram Scripturam* (s.v. *silva*), in *Patrologia Latina*, ed. J.-P. Migne, CXII (Paris: Garnier, 1878).

[66] See Marques Braga's edition of Vicente's *Obras completas* (Lisbon: Sá da Costa, 1951), VI, 132, 133, 161.

Our scene-by-scene examination of this play leads us inevitably to the conclusion that a close-knit dramatic coherence, as we tend to understand it today, is wanting. This is not to say, however, that the various scenes are entirely disconnected. It is hoped that their relationship, in terms of theme and function, has now been made clear. As in Gil Vicente's theater in general, the scenes, considered individually, pose no problem as to unity. Even Giuseppe Tavani, who otherwise maintains that all of Gil Vicente's plays lack unity, admits that the scenes *per se* are "drammaticamente perfette." [67]

The play as a whole exhibits the kind of structure which typifies pageantry. There is a comic superstructure, to which all the elements utilized in this play are made to conform, and which corresponds, as already pointed out, to the playwright's intention of providing a *fiesta de alegría*. The use of irony, caricature, satire, parody, disguise, etc., has been instrumental in the realization of the playwright's purpose.

With respect to theme, this is fundamentally a play on human folly, and, more precisely, folly which is based on deceit. The comic nature of such a basis is intensified by a sort of mirror effect: whoever consciously attempts to deceive others suffers the consequences of his own deceit. We have, then, a play about the contrast between appearance and reality, a theme which was to find its full expression later in the baroque writers. In what way does Vicente's treatment of it differ from theirs? The baroque writers conceive the world as deceptive; the basis of Calderón's *La vida es sueño*, for instance, is that things are not what they appear to be; but the question of what is reality is perhaps more explicitly raised in Cervantes' masterpiece, where Don Quijote repeatedly projects his own misunderstanding of reality —as in the episode of the windmills— whereas in the Duke's castle he is presented with a false reality. In the *Floresta*, however, the distance between appearance and reality is the result of human will, the

---

[67] See the Introduction to his edition of the *Comédia de Rubena* (Rome: Ateneo, 1965), p. 18. Also, A. E. Beau, "Gil Vicente: O aspecto 'medieval'...," pp. 139-40.

desire to deceive someone else. Vicente's, then, is not a metaphysical but an ethical point. Many persons are deceived in the play, but all the deceits, with a single exception, are deliberately contrived, and if most of them are successful, it is only because their victims want to be deceived. The usurer, for example, sees an opportunity for profit; his greed leads him to try to deceive the "widow," and thus he lets himself be deceived in turn. His symptoms are shared by the Chief Justice and Cupid.

Organically linked to the theme of deception is that of love or, at least, of love as desire; in effect, whether oriented toward money —as in the case of the usurious merchant— or toward a woman— which is the case with the Chief Justice and Cupid— desire serves as the point of departure for the various fraudulent intrigues, and is eventually frustrated in all cases. The succession of deceits and counterdeceits follows closely the pattern established by folk wisdom: "Es justa razón engañar al engañador."[68] The counterdeceivers, i.e., the disguised squire, the servant girl and Grata Celia, function, though unwittingly, as God's retributive agents. Their case is analogous to those of the Conde Julián, who, in inviting the Moors to Spain to avenge his daughter's dishonor, was carrying out God's will though he thought he acted on his own,[69] and of the Moors, who, in their victory over the Portuguese in the Battle of Alcázarquivir, served unknowingly to administer divine justice.[70] In this light, the Prince's words ("Dios tiene limitado / todo aquello que se haze" — 1197-1198) acquire special importance, for they may suggest that both the deceits and the ruses which defeat them are part of God's plan to open the eyes of the would-be deceiver, so that deceit does not triumph in the end.

Besides being the motivating force in the complication of the situation, love is also the principal ingredient that has gone into character delineation. The craftiness of the male characters, which

---

[68] Correas, *Vocabulario*, pp. 208, 255.
[69] See Menéndez Pidal's *Reliquias de la poesía épica española* (Madrid: Espasa-Calpe, 1951), pp. 7-19.
[70] According to Herrera, God's wrath was brought upon the Portuguese because they had set out on their mission primarily for the sake of spoils; see "Por la pérdida del rey Don Sebastián," in Fernando de Herrera, *Poesías*, ed. Vicente García de Diego (Madrid: Espasa-Calpe, 1914), pp. 80-88.

is the effect of love, is foiled, in each case, by the shrewdness of the female ones, feigned or real. In many of his plays, Vicente demonstrates an enviable talent in the creation of superbly vivid female characters who dominate the stage. Such is the case here. Psychological insight is not lacking, as can be seen primarily in the cases of the "widow," of the young girl who makes the justice ridiculous, and even of Grata Celia.

The set of characters that appears in this play is reminiscent of Vicente's earlier works; most of them have appeared at least once before: Cupid in the *Frágoa de amor* and in the *Nau de amores*; Apollo in the *Templo de Apolo*; the usurer in the *Barca do inferno*; princes from exotic lands are also present in *Rubena* and in the *Nau de amores* and have been assigned roles similar to that of the Prince in this play; a duke is among the saved ones in the *Barca da Glória*; the judge reminds us of the *Juiz da Beira* and of the figure of the Justiça in the *Frágoa*; *velhas*, *môças*, *parvos* and shepherds abound in Vicente's theater.

Apart from the characters, nearly everything recognizably Vicentine has been incorporated in the *Floresta*. If Vicente's theater as a whole is "un cosmos en miniatura," in Dámaso Alonso's terms,[71] then this play can be looked upon as a reflection in miniature of his theater. A distinctive feature of Vicente's development as a dramatist is precisely that he tends to be cyclic; there is no straight line of development, for he constantly experiments with new possibilities.[72] Though the chronology of all his plays has not yet been definitively established, one can easily notice that the transitions from subject to subject are rather brusque: from his early pastoral plays he quickly shifts to the farces; later in his career, he returns to the pastoral with the *Auto pastoril português* and again, much later, with *Mofina Mendes*. His romantic comedies, begun in 1512 with the *Velho da horta*, are separated by a variety of plays on other subjects (his last one, *Amadis de Gaula*, belongs to 1533). He frequently takes up a certain theme and

---

[71] See the Introduction to his edition of *Poesías de Gil Vicente* (Mexico: Seneca, 1940), p. 16.

[72] See Bruce Wardropper, "Approaching the Metaphysical Sense of Gil Vicente's Chivalric Tragicomedies," *BCom*, 16 (Spring 1964), 4; and Eugenio Asensio, "Las fuentes de las *Barcas*," p. 209.

then abandons it, only to come back to it later on. [73] The motif of the lecherous old man, for example, was first introduced by Vicente in the *Velho da horta*; it appeared later in the *Comédia de Rubena* (1521) and again, for the last time, in the *Floresta*. Even when he is not writing plays of shepherds — as at the beginning of his career — shepherds still appear in his later plays, including the *Floresta*, and display comparable features (in this play, the *pastor* still appears clad in sheepskins, keeps alluding to the things that comprise his world, displays crude mannerisms, misapprehends the situation, and draws attention to his sad condition). The same is true of the fools (cf. the ones in the *Barca do inferno*, *Rubena*, *Serra da estrêla*, *Auto da festa*, *Floresta*, etc.). It is because of all this that, as one approaches Vicente's later works, things become more and more complex and not easy to systematize; he seems reluctant to waste anything that may still have dramatic or lyrical potentialities.

It seems hardly necessary to point out that Vicente does not confine himself to any strict notion of historical perspective. The *Floresta* is indeed an indiscriminate mixture of times, places, and personages: the philosopher had advised the ancient Romans but he is still obedient to the *Coleo Romano*; the Chief Justice, who studied in Paris, is in the service of the King of Thessaly; the Prince of *Gran Grecia* is the son of the King of Hungary, and Grata Celia will become Queen of *Persia Mayor*; [74] among those in the company of the Prince, is the Consul of Venice. There are also references to Portugal, Peru, to Abraham, the Church fathers, saints, the Spanish language, etc. While roles have been assigned to Apollo and Cupid, there are frequent allusions to the Christian God. Such lack of perspective is a more or less constant feature in Vicente's theater (in the *Auto da sibila Casandra*, to mention only one, Biblical characters, such as Solomon, Isaiah, Abraham, Moses, appear togeher with the ancient sibyls Erutea, Peresica, Cimeria, and the Trojan Cassandra), and in consonance with the

---

[73] Asensio, ibid.

[74] One would think along with Enzio di Poppa Vólture — see his translation of Vicente's *Teatro* (Florence: Sansoni, 1957), I, 680, n. 2 — that it would be more logical to have "Grecia" instead of "Persia" since Grata Celia is to marry the Prince of Greece. Vicente's general inconsistency in such matters, however, is no guarantee that this is necessary.

medieval tradition. "The storied porticos of the cathedrals and the stages of the medieval plays," writes Joseph Gillet, "are crowded with the worthies of the Bible, those of mythology and legend and of Greek and Roman history, in fraternal confusion." [75]

The variety of materials interwoven in the *Floresta* is reconciled in such a manner that it enhances greatly the comic tone, which is established and maintained essentially through a chain of contrasts, contrasts of characters and attitudes, of levels of speech, and of situations. Comedy, moreover, does not prove by any means incompatible with the seriousness of the moral theme. Mestre Gil then has crowned his career as a dramatist with a play which not only does full justice to his opulent artistic genius, but also reflects the efforts of a thirty-four-year long artistic activity. With the *Floresta de Enganos* the curtain falls to allow for the change of scenery required by the act which is to follow, the *comedia* of the Spanish Golden Age. The echo of the laughter of the audience in King John III's Court can still be heard.

SOME ANTECEDENTS OF THE *Floresta*

> No es el artista un dios que cree de la nada. Lo mismo que hereda un vocabulario y una lengua, hereda un material imaginativo, un lenguaje de la creación artística. Esta cantera sirve indiferentemente al arquitecto genial y al adocenado, pero condiciona las proporciones y traza del edificio. [76]

Gil Vicente's cultural background has been a matter of controversy, but it is generally agreed that his theater had no real predecessors in Portugal. [77] Because of the absence of documentary evidence concerning the existence of a written theatrical tradition before him, one is forced to admit that it was Vicente who

---

[75] In *"Propalladia" and Other Works of Bartolomé de Torres Naharro*, IV (Philadelphia: Univ. of Penn. Press, 1961), 118.

[76] Asensio, "Las fuentes de las *Barcas*," p. 208.

[77] Waldron, *Amadís*, p. 5; see also Dámaso Alonso's edition of Vicente's *Tragicomedia de Don Duardos* (Madrid: Consejo Superior de Investigaciones Científicas, 1942). Ia, 27.

fathered the literary theater in Portugal.[78] This is not to say, however, that he created it *ab ovo*,[79] nor that he was a peculiarly Portuguese phenomenon isolated from general European culture. "La sua cultura," writes Luciana Stegagno Picchio, "è fruto di una lunga maturazione e in essa intervengono tutti i motivi che hanno formato la grande cultura europea dell'età di mezzo; il suo teatro non è punto di partenza ma, come tutte le grandi creazioni, un punto d'arrivo, una *summa* nel senso medievale della parola."[80]

To seek sources which might have inspired Vicente is not to deny him originality, as some of his compatriots seem inclined to believe: by the standards prevalent in his days, originality was not a question of theme but rather of the manner in which the theme was treated, and imitation was in no way to be condemned.[81]

Scholars have pointed out a few literary antecedents, of varying degrees of resemblance to the *Floresta*, with which Vicente may have been familiar, though we should not forget Eugenio Asensio's words that "sólo cuando está atestiguado el hecho histórico de la transmisión o cuando las semejanzas se amontonan, puede afirmarse con cierta seguridad el contacto directo."[82]

Georges LeGentil has traced the points of contact between the sixteenth-century French morality *Dialogue du fol et du sage* and the introductory scene of the *Floresta*, and also between the *Sottie des trompeurs* (performed in 1530) and the episode of the merchant.[83]

---

[78] I. S. Révah, "Gil Vicente a-t-il été le fondateur du théâtre portugais?," *BHTP*, 1 (1950), 168, 170, 182.

[79] See António José Saraiva, *Gil Vicente e o fim do teatro medieval*, 2nd ed. (Lisbon: Europa-América, 1965), pp. 205 ff.

[80] "Il *Pater Noster* dell'*Auto do Velho da Horta*," *AION-SR*, 3 (1961), 198; see also pp. 193-94 as well as her "Diavolo e inferno nel teatro di Gil Vicente," *AION-SR*, 1 (1959), 33-34 and 39, and her "*Arremedilho*. Di un presunto componimento drammatico giullaresco alle origini del teatro portoghese," *AION-SR*, 2 (1960), 31-32.

[81] Stegagno Picchio, "Il *Pater Noster*," p. 194; C.-H. Frèches, *Le Théâtre neo-latin au Portugal: 1550-1745* (Paris: A. G. Nizet, 1964), p. 30.

[82] "El soneto 'No me mueve, mi Dios...' y un auto vicentino inspirados en Santa Catalina de Siena," *RFE*, 34 (1950), 136.

[83] See his "Les thèmes de Gil Vicente dans les moralités, sotties et farces françaises," in *Hommage à Ernest Martinenche* (Paris: Editions d'Artrey, n.d.), pp. 163 ff.

The mythological episode has been considered a variant of the story of Cupid and Psyche.[84] Indeed, there is a good deal of resemblance between them. The first known version of the romance of Cupid and Psyche forms part of Apuleius' *Metamorphoses* or *Asinus Aureus*. After Apuleius, the story became very popular and exercised a considerable literary influence. It was imitated by Martianus Capella in the fifth century in his encyclopedia of the seven liberal arts; in the following century, the grammarian Fulgentius Planciades retold it briefly and supplied it with a long allegorical explication in his *Mythology*. We do not know for certain whether the *Metamorphoses* was known outside of Italy between the sixth century and the thirteenth; but similarities to the Psyche story have been seen in certain medieval French romances, namely *Parténopeus de Blois*, the *Chevalier au cygne* and *Huon de Bordeaux*, and in a Middle High German poem, *Friedrich von Schwaben*.[85] In Italy, there is a late medieval manuscript tradition of the *Metamorphoses*; the first known manuscript — now in the Laurentian Library in Florence — belongs to the eleventh century; the work was copied at least once in the twelfth century and several times in the thirteenth. It was Giovanni Boccaccio who made Apuleius' novel known.[86] From his time until the nineteenth century, the *Metamorphoses* exerted a profound influence and the story of Cupid and Psyche served as inspiration for numerous literary creations.[87] The first printed edition of Apuleius, by Giovanni Andrea de Bussi, dates from 1469 (Rome).[88] The first Spanish translation is Diego López de Cortegana's; its first printed edition is without place or date but Menéndez y Pelayo and others locate it in Seville, 1513.[89] The book was quite popular in Spain during the sixteenth and

---

[84] See Aubrey Bell, *Gil Vicente*, p. 53, and *Portuguese Literature*, p. 119. Bell does not go beyond stating the fact.

[85] Elizabeth H. Haight, *Apuleius and His Influence* (New York: Longmans, Green and Co., 1927), Ch. iv, and her *More Essays on Greek Romances* (New York: Longmans, Green and Co., 1945), Ch. v. See also Jan-Öjvind Swahn, *The Tale of Cupid and Psyche* (Lund: CWK Gleerup, 1955), pp. 382-84.

[86] Haight, *Apuleius*, p. 112.

[87] Ibid.

[88] Ibid., p. 92.

[89] See Menéndez y Pelayo, *Bibliografía hispano-latina clásica*, I (Santander: Aldus, 1950). 85-86.

seventeenth centuries, and was reprinted several times.[90] The tale of Cupid and Psyche was also separately adapted and imitated by numerous writers, poets and dramatists in particular, ranging from Juan de la Cueva to Lope and Calderón — not to mention later ones.[91] Carolina Michaëlis — who, incidentally, does not mention the influence of this tale on the *Floresta* — argues that the origin of Vicente's knowledge of it should be sought in Boccaccio rather than in Apuleius.[92] In addition to writing a copy of the *Metamorphoses* in his own hand, Boccaccio recapitulated, in condensed form, the Cupid and Psyche romance and gave it an allegorical interpretation, in his *Genealogia deorum gentilium* (1372), a mythological encyclopedia in Latin prose.[93] His treatment of the story differs from Apuleius' in the following respects: "first, the characterization of Psyche's sisters... is omitted.... Second, Psyche's tasks and the miraculous forms of aid given to her to complete them are not described. And third, the part of the Olympian gods in the story is greatly minimized."[94] The *Genealogia* won immediate success and circulated widely, as is shown by the large number of manuscript and printed editions both in Italy and elsewhere; first printed in Venice in 1472, it underwent seven subsequent editions including one in Paris (1511).[95] For two centuries the *Genealogia* served as the "central storehouse from which educated men drew their knowledge of the gods."[96] Arturo Farinelli affirms that already toward the end of the fourteenth century, Boccaccio's works were introduced to

---

[90] Ibid., pp. 91 ff. In his *Orígenes de la novela*, NBAE, 21 (1915), Menéndez y Pelayo includes the text of the Medina del Campo edition (1543) of this translation. The story of Cupid and Psyche extends from Ch. v of Bk. IV to Ch. iii of Bk. VI.
[91] Menéndez y Pelayo, *Bibliografía*, I, 98 ff.
[92] *Notas vicentinas*, p. 322, n. 264.
[93] Haight, *Apuleius*, pp. 119-20, and *More Essays*, pp. 113-14. For the text, see Vincenzo Romano's edition (Bari: G. Laterza, 1951), Vol. I, Bk. V, Ch. xxii: "De Psyce XVa Apollinis filia."
[94] Haight, *More Essays*, p. 136.
[95] See Ernest H. Wilkins, *The University of Chicago Manuscript of the "Genealogia Deorum Gentilium" of Boccaccio* (Chicago: Univ. of Chicago Press, 1927), pp. 4-6, and his "The Genealogy of the Editions of the Genealogia Deorum," MP, 17 (1919), 425-38. Carolina Michaëlis, (*Notas*, p. 336, n. 312) thinks that the Paris edition may have served as source for Vicente.
[96] Jean Seznec, *The Survival of the Pagan Gods*, trans. Barbara F. Sessions (New York: Harper and Row, 1961), p. 224.

Spain "dove, coi militi, i mercanti, il corteo dei principi, che in Italia s'eran fatta un'appendice di regno, fonte di guai, passano i frutti della coltura, italiana, passano i codici, passano i poemi e le storie, passa la scienza vecchia e nuova, immagazzinata nei libri." [97] His Latin writings were diffused primarily among ecclesiastics who had a command of Latin. [98] The fifteenth century saw several imitations and manuscript translations of the *Genealogia* into Spanish. Among the books of the Marqués de Santillana was Martín de Ávila's translation of it — formerly attributed to Pero Díaz de Toledo. [99] Of this or of one of the other translations "bem pode ser viesse cópia para a Livraria de Afonso V. Porventura por intervenção do Condestável D. Pedro, que apaixonado pelo espírito novo do *Renascimento,* utilizou amplamente nos seus doutos poemas o estilo dantesco e a obra tôda de Bocácio, que tinha o seu lugar na preciosa livraria dêle." [100]

It is not unlikely, then, that Vicente was familiar with the story of Cupid and Psyche. There is also ample evidence that the story contains elements which have existed in popular tradition; Stith Thompson and other folklorists have recorded several separate motifs and variants, such as: personal offences against gods punished; [101] child sacrificed to gain favor of gods (S263.2); [102] father casts daughter forth (S322.1); banishment (exile) as punishment (Q431); [103] abandonment on mountain (S147); whirlwind carries princess away (R17.1); child of deity visits earth (F31); marriage of mortal and supernatural being (T111); [104] disenchantment (transformation) by breaking tabu (D789.4 and D510 ff); [105] tasks, tests, quests (H900-H1399); [106] animals (extraordinary companions) perform hero's tasks (B571 ff, and F601.1). Jan-Öjvind

---

[97] *Italia e Spagna* (Turin: Fratelli Bocca, 1929), I, 100-01.
[98] Ibid., p. 99.
[99] See Jules Piccus, "El traductor español de *De Genealogia Deorum,*" in *Homenaje a Rodríguez-Moñino* (Madrid: Castalia, 1966), II, 59-75.
[100] Carolina Michaëlis, *Notas,* p. 336.
[101] Stith Thompson, *Motif-Index,* Q221.
[102] Cf. also John E. Keller, *Motif-Index of Mediaeval Spanish Exempla,* S263.2.3.
[103] Also, Ralph S. Boggs, *Index of Spanish Folktales,* FF Communications, No. 90 (Helsinki: Academia Scientiarum Fennica, 1930), nos. 705-09.
[104] And Boggs, nos. 425-49.
[105] See also Keller, C960.
[106] Also, Boggs, nos. 460-99.

Swahn has composed a more detailed list of pertinent motifs and sub-types from general folklore and, separately, from Portuguese and Hispanic;[107] they all, however, revolve around the central motifs of (1) the Supernatural Husband, (2) the Marriage, (3) the Breaking of the Tabu, (4) the Search for the Vanished Husband, and (5) the Reunion. Moreover, in the majority of them, as in Apuleius but not as in Vicente's play, the emphasis is on the supernatural or on magic. It should also be noted that most of the aforementioned five general motifs are lacking in the *Floresta*. It would, therefore, be daring to assume that by piecing together — without any knowledge of the Psyche story itself — these individual folk elements, Vicente succeeded in reconstructing the story to the extent he did. It seems more plausible to argue that he knew the story and blended traditional motifs with it. Popular tradition may also have offered him certain motifs, which, though not directly related to the story of Cupid and Psyche, are recognizable in his version, especially in the second part; the following are among them:

—dragon keeps maiden tied with golden chain (B11.10.1);
—deception into allowing oneself to be fettered (K713);
—rescue of princess from mountain (R111.2.2);
—prince accidentally finds maiden and marries her (N711).

Examined in the light of his possible literary sources, Vicente's dramatization of the tale parallels Apuleius' version—or Boccaccio's retelling of it — in several respects; a comparison of the three versions will show that Vicente has retained many of the basic features, such as: the princess Psyche's extraordinary beauty (lines 804-817, 882, 1008); Venus' wrath (in the *Floresta* it is the wrath of the goddesses Verecinta, Juno and Pallas: 410-414); Cupid's love for Psyche (281 ff); the king's visit to Apollo's temple (380-381); Apollo's advice that the king should take his daugther to a mountain and abandon her there (426-434); the king's despair (the queen's, too, in the two older versions: 444 ff); Psyche's effort to console her father (her parents in the original: 458-468); the king's compliance with the will of the god (747

---

[107] *The Tale of Cupid and Psyche*, pp. 24-36, 162-64, and 168-74.

ff); Psyche abandoned on the mountain; her distress (770-778, 788-791, 837-843); the divine intervention in the end (it is Jupiter who intervenes in Apuleius and Boccaccio, Ventura in Vicente: 1148 ff). The other details of Vicente's version, however, are different, and a large portion of the story is omitted in the *Floresta*. In the original, Venus' wrath springs from jealousy of Psyche's beauty; in Vicente, the goddesses' wrath is prompted by Grata Celia's reputed evil-doings. In the original, Cupid is sent to Psyche by Venus as an agent of revenge, whereas in the *Floresta* he pursues Grata Celia for his own sake. Psyche is aware of what awaits her but Grata Celia is not. Psyche is married to, and falls in love with Cupid; Grata Celia rejects Cupid's love and is married to the Prince of Greece. Besides, Vicente has enriched his adaptation of the tale with other elements, namely courtly love, deceitful intrigues, the comic scene of the shepherd, the closing scene with Ventura, etc. His indebtedness to the Psyche story can be seen primarily in the first part of the mythological episode.

Into his adaptation of this tale, Vicente has also interwoven the dramatically most intense scene of the story of Abraham and Isaac. The resemblance of the latter to his version of the story of Cupid and Psyche in situation as well as tone is striking: Telebano's submission to Apollo's command and the profundity of his pain as a father; Grata Celia's initial ignorance of her destiny and her concern for her father's grief; their departure and arrival at the mountain, and her reaction to the disclosure of the bad news, all have their counterparts in the Old Testament story. In this case, the playwright has explicitly revealed the source he has utilized (TELEBANO: "Como hizo Abrahán, / hago sacreficio de vos" — 759-760). To try to establish the exact source of Vicente's knowledge of the story would be superfluous; it was so popular throughout the Middle Ages that it would have been next to impossible for it "to escape the eyes and ears of anybody, however uninterested he might be in it."[108] Owing principally to its figural quality (Isaac's sacrifice prefigures Christ's), it was exten-

---

[108] Rosemary Woolf, "The Effect of Typology on the English Mediaeval Plays of Abraham and Isaac," *Speculum*, 32 (1957), 806.

sively referred to in all kinds of religious works and depicted on stained glass, carving, painting and manuscript illumination.[109]

The episode of the Chief Justice, finally, bears resemblance to the seventeenth of the *Cent nouvelles nouvelles*, a major monument of fifteenth-century French literature.[110] This work, generally attributed to Antoine de la Sale, must have been compiled between 1456 and 1461. Written to entertain one of the wealthiest and culturally most outstanding court circles in Europe, that of Duke Philip of Burgundy, it soon became very popular: in the first hundred years after its printing in 1486, it went into eleven editions.[111] The great number of similarities, both in situation and characterization, between its seventeenth story and the scene under discussion in the *Floresta* makes it clear that Vicente had either read or heard the story: the male protagonist's association with the exercise of law (he is the President of the Chancery Court at Paris, in the French story); cf. lines 472-473; his learning (487-488, 740); his amorous inclinations despite his advanced age and the fact that he is married (515-516, 531-533); his infatuation with a young girl (one of the maids of his own household, in the *Cent nouvelles*); 702-705, 737-740; the maid's baking bread (588-589); his manner of enticing her (he makes generous propositions); 546-550; her determination not to submit to his advances (567-569); the scene in the room where the maid is sifting flour (in the French story, the old man attacks her); 577 ff; the shrewd ruse she employs in her defense and the manner in which she carries it out (599 ff); her making him disguise himself as a woman and sift flour (600-602); his wife's rebuke (assigned to the old lady in the *Floresta*): "Ha! maistre, et qu'est cecy? Où sont voz lettres, voz grans honneurs, voz sciences et discrecions?"[112] (672-676, 686-688, 690-701).

Vicente's dramatization, besides being more elaborate than the French story, has gained much, in terms of theatricality, by his

---

[109] Ibid., p. 806 and ff.
[110] Aubrey Bell (*Estudos vicentinos*, p. 110) has pointed out the source of inspiration for this episode without going into any further details.
[111] See the Introduction to *The Hundred Tales*, trans. R. H. Robbins (New York: Crown Publishers, 1960).
[112] *Les cent nouvelles nouvelles*, ed. Paul Lacroix (Paris: G. Charpentier, 1884), p. 95.

accentuation of the farcical tone and the introduction of additional motifs, such as the Judge's whistling to gain admission to the maid's house, his Negro jargon, the *velha*'s more extensive and severe verbal attack, and his unsuccessful attempt to recover his clothes.

Here again, we should perhaps add that some of the motifs are traditional. Stith Thompson registers a few which are related either to both the French story and Vicente's adaptation, or to the latter alone:

—disguise of man in woman's dress (K1836);
—man in danger of life dressed by hostess as woman and set to baking (K521.4.1.2);
—man gulled into giving up his clothes (K330.1).

There are also echoes, in the general shape of the Chief Justice episode, of the legend of Aristotle and Phyllis, so widely diffused in medieval and later iconography and writings, and so frequently utilized in sermons for its moralistic potential.[113] The nucleus of the tale — an impassioned wise man beguiled and persuaded by a damsel into letting her ride him on all-fours — is of oriental origin; it occurs both in early Indian stories and in Arabic literature; the application to Aristotle is a later invention of western Europe. Two versions of it, one French, the other German, belong to the first half of the thirteenth century. In its original form, the story served to illustrate the malicious and dangerous powers of women and, of course, the omnipotence of love. Once applied to Aristotle, its didactic potential increased so as to include a lesson about the vanity of pagan learning. Given the medieval cult of Aristotle, it is easy to see how powerful an argument the preachers had at their disposal.[114] Since the tale was so widely known, there is little doubt that Vicente had access to it. A written source which may have inspired him is Alfonso Martínez de Toledo's condensed version in the *Cor-*

---

[113] George Sarton, "Aristotle and Phyllis," *Isis*, 14 (1930), 8-19, and Émile Mâle, *L'art religieux du XIIIe siècle en France* (Paris: Armand Colin, 1925), pp. 337-38. Sarton's study includes plates also. See also Stith Thompson, K1215, and Boggs, no. 1424.

[114] Sarton, pp. 9-11.

bacho,[115] several times reprinted in Vicente's lifetime.[116] A possible further testimony to Vicente's knowledge of the legend is the final scene of *Inês Pereira* (1523), where the heroine literally rides on Pero Marques' back.[117] That the playwright does in the *Floresta* something he had done thirteen years earlier in *Inês* should not be surprising, for, as already pointed out, he often returned to materials he had used before and presented them in a new light. The similarities between this scene of the *Floresta* and the medieval tale are not so explicit nor so exact as in *Inês*: the Chief Justice is ridden by the *môça* only in a metaphorical sense. Unlike Pero Marques, however, the Chief Justice is portrayed as a very learned man indeed, and, like Aristotle, as the king's right hand — it is to him that the king delegates authority during his absence. Also, both the Justice and Aristotle are presented as victims of what the author of the *Corbacho* calls "loco e desordenado amor."

Here Vicente seems to have exploited the legend primarily for its comic possibilities, without, of course, failing to show the negative power of untimely love, a theme he had elaborated a quarter of a century before in the *Velho da horta*. Naturally, the wiser the lover, the greater the ridicule; in this sense, Aristotle's sorry failure prefigures that of the Justice.

Vicente's adroit synthesis in the *Floresta* of elements from a wide range of sources has produced a play which is both his own and a *summa*, in the medieval sense of the term. His dependence upon his sources is not servile; he has used them only insofar as they have enabled him to reach his own, often quite different, ends; and when necessary, he has digressed from them. All the ingredients he has borrowed and those he has supplied himself are subordinated to, and unified mainly by the central

---

[115] See Lesley Byrd Simpson's edition (Berkeley: Univ. of Calif. Press, 1939), pp. 53-54.

[116] There were at least five editions of the *Corbacho* in the dramatist's lifetime (Seville, 1498; Toledo, 1499, 1500, 1518; and Logroño, 1529); see Menéndez y Pelayo, *Orígenes de la novela*, NBAE, 1 (1905), cvii (note). See also F. J. Norton, *Printing in Spain: 1501-1520* (Cambridge: Cambridge Univ. Press, 1966), p. 45, and Clara Louisa Penney, *List of Books Printed before 1601* (New York: Hispanic Society of America, 1929), p. 160.

[117] This parallel has been developed by Thomas R. Hart in his "La estructura dramática del *Auto de Inês Pereira*," *NRFH*, 18 (1965-1966), 165, n. 8.

elements of comedy and satire, and they serve to reinforce the impression of the deceivers' just failure. The *Cent nouvelles nouvelles* has furnished him the foundation upon which he has developed the Chief Justice episode. His genius has produced three characters so full of life that it is really difficult to decide which is the protagonist, and has led him well beyond the limits of his model, toward the complete ridicule of the Justice. Each line, while bringing the Justice closer to his downfall, heightens the atmosphere of comedy. The same atmosphere, though admittedly subdued, envelops the mythological episode, and is not harmed even by the introduction of the Old Testament story of Abraham's sacrifice of Isaac, since the spectator, or the reader, already knows that the imminent catastrophe has only been contrived by Cupid to aid his plan of conquering Grata Celia. The irony is, however, that Apollo's false oracle is substantiated in the end when Grata Celia finds in the *floresta* her *dicha mayor*. Among the major ingredients which the playwright has supplied of his own, apart from the intricate interweaving of deceits, is courtly love or, more accurately, the parody of it, by means of which both the Justice and Cupid are rendered highly comic.

The Linguistic Texture of the *Floresta*

The *Floresta de Enganos* is one of Gil Vicente's bilingual plays, composed partly in Spanish and partly in Portuguese; if one wishes to take account of a few words and phrases in Latin, macarronic in some cases, it is a trilingual play.[118] Problematic though it may appear today, bilingualism must not have obstructed representation in any way. When composing, the playwright did not have posterity or even, presumably, publication in mind;

---

[118] Eighteen of his plays are bilingual; eleven are entirely in Spanish and fifteen in Portuguese. Two anonymous plays, the *Auto da geraçam humana* and the *Auto de Deus padre e Justiça e Misericórdia*, which have been attributed to Gil Vicente by I. S. Révah, are not counted here. In terms of the number of lines composed in each language, two thirds of the dramatist's work is written in Portuguese and the remaining third in Spanish; see Paul Teyssier, *La langue de Gil Vicente* (Paris: Klincksieck, 1959), p. 296.

his dramatic activity was confined to a particular time (the first third of the sixteenth century) and a particular place (the "hispanized" Portuguese royal Court). The courtly audience would have had no difficulty in understanding what was said on the stage. For both Vicente and his audience the mixture of the two languages must have appeared natural. [119]

Albin E. Beau holds that "no se descubren... principios rigurosamente observados y consecuentemente aplicados," in the distribution of Spanish and Portuguese in Vicente's dramatic production. [120] In fact there are inconsistencies even within the same play (e.g., Melidonio speaks both Spanish and Portuguese in the *Devisa da cidade de Coimbra*, 1527). An examination of the linguistic texture of the *Floresta* will reinforce Beau's view. The major portion of the play is in Spanish. The philosopher and the simpleton of the opening scene speak this language; so do the pagan gods, Apollo and Cupid, King Telebano and his daughter Grata Celia, the Chief Justice of Telebano's kingdom, Ventura, the Prince of Greece and the Duke. With the exception of the first two, all the Spanish-speaking characters are involved in one way or another in the romantic episode which forms the basis of the play's structure; as Paul Teyssier has indicated, Spanish "deviendra dans Gil Vicente la langue de la comédie romanesque." [121] The remaining personages, that is the merchant, the Squire disguised as a widow, the old woman, the shepherd, and the two servant girls, speak Portuguese. In some cases, there may be a combination of explanations for the characters' use of Spanish. Cupid, for instance, may speak Spanish because he is a pagan god, [122] or because he is caricatured as a courtly lover. [123] But why should the Prince and the Duke speak Spanish? First, because they are noblemen (according to Teyssier's principle of linguistic hierarchy, Spanish had come to be "une langue distinguée et noble, celle des cercles élevés de la cour, des ambassadeurs, des princes,

---

[119] Ibid., p. 297.
[120] "El bilingüismo en Gil Vicente," *StPh*, 1 (1960), 222, *et passim*.
[121] Teyssier, p. 298.
[122] Spanish was assigned to imaginary figures; see Teyssier, p. 299, and Aubrey Bell, *Gil Vicente*, p. 20.
[123] The same could be said of the Chief Justice. An analogous case is that of the Spaniard in the *Auto da Fama*.

des reines," whereas Portuguese had a more popular quality [124]); second, because they are foreigners, [125] and third, because they are imaginary figures — though to a lesser degree than Cupid — within an imaginary framework. [126] It is clear that the Portuguese-speaking characters belong to a lower social class than the Spanish-speaking ones; yet, why should the *parvo* speak Spanish? None of the views expounded about Vicente's motives in distributing the two languages can explain this discrepancy, unless, of course, one wishes to call to one's aid Beau's idea of the nationality of the actors. Since Vicente looked ahead to representation, it is likely, Beau believes, that when writing each part, Vicente had to consider the mother tongue of each available actor. [127] There is, however, no evidence to support an assumption that the actor who played the *parvo* was a Spaniard. Teyssier sees this particular problem as an example of Gil Vicente's dependence on the literary tradition: "Gil Vicente se souvient du théâtre espagnol qui, depuis quelques années, avait créé le type comique du *Bobo*." [128] This solution, however, is not really tenable, for in 1536 the character of the *bobo* was not yet quite developed in Spanish literature. True, there had been traits, which would eventually blend to form this character as he appears in the theater of Lope de Rueda, even in the *Libro de buen amor* (cf. "la disputaçión que los griegos é los romanos en uno ovieron"); but we can hardly speak of the *bobo* as an already conventional character who might have influenced Gil Vicente. Rather, it would be logical to argue that Vicente's *parvo*, who had apeared earlier in his theater (for example in the *Auto da barca do inferno*, 1517), anticipates the later *bobo*. The case of the *parvo* in the *Floresta*, then, serves as additional testimony for the lack of definite criteria in selecting one language rather than the other.

That Gil Vicente should use Spanish, in addition to his own language, is not at all surprising: his is not an isolated case in the letters of Portugal, but the reflection of a much wider and more

---

[124] *La langue*, p. 300. See also Bell, *Gil Vicente*, pp. 19-21.
[125] Bell (ibid., and *Estudos vicentinos*, p. 33) declares that Spanish was the language assigned to a foreigner.
[126] See *supra*, note 122.
[127] Op. cit., pp. 222-23.
[128] *La langue*, p. 298.

general phenomenon.[129] In the *Floresta*, as in all his works, his Spanish has its own idiosyncrasies. Menéndez y Pelayo had pointed out that it was typical of one who had never been in Castile.[130] It is characterized, as Dámaso Alonso affirms, by "vacilación" and "titubeo", both of which are natural results of the fact that Vicente stood

> en la encrucijada de los vientos, en la encrucijada de su portugués nativo, su leonés inicial, su castellano sobrepuesto; en la división de las aguas del castellano medieval y el clásico, entrecruzada aun con la del portugués medieval y el clásico; en el punto de choque de una gran tradición literaria castellana, con una modesta, sí, pero familiar, tradición castellanizante portuguesa.[131]

But Alonso concludes that fortunately "portuguesismo, leonesismo y arcaísmo castellano tienen con frecuencia una frontera borrosa, y a quien haya leído literatura medieval española muchas de estas irregularidades no le han de producir embarazo."[132]

Here again Vicente exhibits the same general tendency typifying the Portuguese authors who wrote in Spanish. In the course

---

[129] During the second half of the fifteenth century, Portugal's relations with Castile became increasingly intimate, thanks primarily to the intermarriages between the royal families of the two countries. These events had a telling effect on the composition of the Portuguese Court, for, along with the Castilian princesses, there was a considerable influx of Castilians. As a consequence the Court became bilingual. Castilian, then, came to be a sign of social prestige, a status symbol. Spoken among the aristocratic circles of the time, it was considered "la langue noble, distinguée, raffinée." The fifteenth century was also witness to an unprecedented growth of Castilian literature. This exercised an enormous influence on the Portuguese literati, who not only turned to Castile for literary inspiration and guidance, but also adopted her language; even when writing in their own tongue, they would welcome "les habitudes, les goûts, le style des Castillans." It should also be remembered that the linguistic distance between Spanish and Portuguese was not as wide those days as it is today (see Teyssier, pp. 293-96). Gil Vicente's use of Spanish thus reflects the linguistic habits of his milieu.

[130] In *Antología de poetas líricos castellanos*, VII, clxxxviii.

[131] "Problemas del castellano vicentino," in his edition of the *Tragicomedia de Don Duardos* (Madrid: Consejo Superior de Investigaciones Científicas, 1942), I. Quoted in Waldron's edition of *Amadís*, p. 53.

[132] See the Introduction to his edition of *Don Duardos* (Madrid: Consejo Superior de Investigaciones Científicas, 1942), Ia, 11.

of time, the Spanish practiced in Portugal took on new features until it reached an identity of its own.[133]

NORMS GUIDING THE TRANSCRIPTION OF THE TEXT

It is not only the above peculiarities of Vicente's Spanish that a modern editor has to face. The arbitrariness of all those who had a hand in the preparation of the *editio princeps* of 1562 has produced a text so mutilated that it is impossible to restore it to its original form. Moreover, no two of the half-dozen extant copies of this edition are identical with each other,[134] a fact which can be explained by the proof-correcting practices in the printing of books prior to the nineteenth century:

> special proofs were not usually pulled for... correction before printing. Instead, after only cursory examination the type-pages would be placed on the press and printing started. An early pull would usually be read by some printing-house functionary, who would then stop the press for corrections. As a result, the text of each sheet in early books may exist in two or more states that reflect different stages of the proofreading.[135]

Also when type-pages were accidentally damaged during the printing process, it was possible for variant readings to be mistakenly introduced in the resetting.[136] Unfortunately, things are even worse with the facsimile reproduction of 1928, for, in addition to the errors contained in the prototype, it encompasses many digressions from it. Stephen Reckert has brought to light a large number of errors, which occurred in the preparation of the facsimile.[137] The choice of facsimile process is the main factor responsible for these corruptions: among the three prin-

---

[133] Teyssier, p. 296.

[134] See Stephen Reckert, "El verdadero texto de la *Copilaçam* vicentina de 1562," pp. 54, 67-68.

[135] Fredson Bowers, "Textual Criticism," in *The Aims and Methods of Scholarship in Modern Languages and Literatures,* ed. James Thorpe (New York: MLA, 1968), p. 33.

[136] Ibid., p. 34.

[137] Op. cit.

cipal methods of reproduction (i.e. *collotype, screened offset* and *unscreened* or *line offset*), the editors of the Biblioteca Nacional chose the latter, [138] apparently because it is by far the cheapest. [139] Line offset, as Fredson Bowers has shown, is the least faithful and accurate method since it reproduces no values whatsoever: "everything in the photographed document above a certain intensity registers as black: everything below this level of intensity registers as white." [140] As a result, the negatives have to be retouched by a laboratory technician; but "when manipulation of any kind intervenes as a necessary part of the process of transferring a photographic image of a document to facsimile print, the possibility of abuse of the original by alteration of some kind occurs." [141]

The emendations proposed by Reckert [142] have been taken into account in the preparation of the following text of the *Floresta*, which is based on that of the *Copilaçam* of 1562 as it appears in the facsimile reproduction of 1928. Otherwise, since it is impossible to decide which of the various types of errors contained in the 1562 edition are genuinely Vicente's and which are not, the text has been respected, except for the following points:

(1) abbreviations have been expanded.

(2) the signs & and *z* have been rendered *y* in Spanish and *e* in Portuguese.

(3) the signs introducing the strophes have been omitted and replaced by identation.

(4) old long *s* has been modernized.

(5) punctuation, accentuation and capitalization have been modernized.

(6) *h* has been deleted or added in accordance with modern usage.

---

[138] Ibid., p. 53.
[139] Fredson Bowers, "The Yale Folio Facsimile and Scholarship," *MP*, 53 (1955), 51.
[140] Ibid., p 50.
[141] Ibid.
[142] Op. cit., pp. 60-61.

(7) double consonants have been simplified, unless they indicate a difference in phonetic value (as in the case of intervocalic *ss*).

(8) the graphs *ç, z, x, j*, have been retained because they represented, at the beginning of the sixteenth century, sounds which have not survived in modern Spanish: the sibilant *ç* was pronounced *ts*, as in Italian *forza*; *z* was pronounced *dz*, as in Italian *mezzo*; *x* was an unvoiced pre-palatal fricative similar to the Italian *sc* in *pesce*; *j* was still voiced (like intervocalic *s*), as in Portuguese *janela*.[143]

(9) the etymological graph *ph* has been simplified to *f* (*philosophia* - filosofía, *prophano* - profano).

(10) *u* and *i* with consonantal value have been changed to *v* and *j* respectively; conversely, *v* and *y* have been changed to *u* and *i* when they represent vowels.

(11) double vowels denoting a stressed syllable have been simplified and accents have been added in conformity with modern usage.

(12) whenever *oo* and *aa* (or *haa*) represent exclamations, they have been transcribed *oh* and *ah* respectively.

(13) words joined together have been separated only when necessary to avoid confusion (e.g., "¿por qué?" but *porque*).

(14) the elided *e* of the preposition *de* is indicated by an apostrophe only before a noun or an infinitive (*damores* - d'amores, *dachar* - d'achar, but *desta* - desta).

(15) the few Latin terms in he text have been italicized.

(16) obvious printing errors have been corrected in the text and are found in the notes.

(17) no attempt has been made to introduce textual corrections for the sake of meter or rime.

(18) the occasional occurrence of Portuguese *lh* and *nh* for Spanish *ll* and *ñ*, and vice-versa, has been silently emended since it represents no change in phonetic value.

(19) the foliation, in the right-hand margin, corresponds to that of the 1562 edition; the letters *a, b, c, d* represent the columns of each folio.

---

[143] See Rafael Lapesa, *Historia de la lengua española*, 5th ed. (Madrid: Escelicer, 1959), pp. 146-47.

(20) the names of the characters in the left-hand margin are given in their full Spanish or Portuguese forms, depending on which of the two languages each speaks. The only exception is *Parvo*, a word which in Spanish has a different meaning (its Spanish equivalent is *Bobo*).

(21) the songs have been placed within quotation marks.

TEXT OF THE *FLORESTA DE ENGANOS*

[*fo.* 114 *r*]

Comédia chamada *Floresta d'enganos*. Foi representada ao muito alto e poderoso Rei dom Ioam, o terceiro dêste nome, na sua cidade de Évora. Era do Senhor de MDXXXVI anos.

Figuras dela:

Um FILÓSOFO com um PARVO atado ao pé, um MERCADOR, um homem em trajos de VIÚVA com uma MOCINHA, COPIDO, APOLO, Rei TELEBANO, GRATA CÉLIA (Princesa), DOUTOR (Justiça maior), uma VELHA, um PASTOR, um DUQUE pelegrino, um PRÍNCIPE, a VENTURA pelegrina com outros três PELEGRINOS.

Entra logo o Filósofo, *com o* Parvo *atado ao pé, e diz*:

    Asegún siento mis males,   [*fo*. 114 *a*]
al discreto singular
gran pena le es conversar
con los necios perenales,
sin lo poder escusar.   5
Los muy antigos romanos,
començando a ser tiranos
porque Roma se ofendía,
yo, por mi filosofía,
les di consejos muy sanos.   10
  Y porque la reprehensión
a todos es enojosa,
me vi en grande passión;
y me echaron en prisión,
en cárcel muy tenebrosa.   15
No bastó: mas en depués
daquesto que oído havéis,
sólo por esto que digo,
ataron ansí comigo
este bovo que aquí veis.   20
  Que lo traiga desta suerte
al comer y al cenar,
al dormir y platicar;
esto so pena de muerte
que no lo pueda dexar   25
hasta el morir.

Parvo.   ¿Haste d'ir?
Filósofo.   ¿No me dexarás dezir   [*b*]

	la causa que me ha traído?	
Parvo.	Hasta la mañana.	
Filósofo.	Déxame ora ser oído	30
	desta gente cortesana.	
Parvo.	Mi amo, aquí hablaré yo,	
	y quando en casa estuviéredes	
	hablá quanto vos quisiéredes;	
	que nunca os diré de no,	35
	aunque quebréis las paredes.	
Filósofo.	Habla, por ver qué dirás.	
	¡Oh, quien no sintiesse más	
	de lo malo ni de lo bueno,	
	de lo suyo y de lo ageno,	40
	de quanto tú sentirás!	
	El mi tormento se ve	
	por este exemplo esquierdo:	
	si queréis matar al cuerdo,	
	atalde un necio al pie;	45
	y ansí el seso pierdo.	
	O quiçá vino esto a ser	
	porque no quise casar,	
	con recelo de topar	
	muger de flaco entender,	50
	como se suele acertar.	

Canta o Parvo:

	"Allevánteste, panadera,	
	si te has de llevantar,	
	que un fraile dexo muerto.	
	No traigo vino ni pan.	55
	Apiahá, apiahá, apiahá."	[c]
	Dizid, amo, ¿haste d'ir hoje	
	o hasta la mañana?	
Filósofo.	¿Quién será que no se enoje,	
	y todo mal se le antoje,	60
	de una necedad tamaña?	
	Yo no sé quién sofrirá	
	v a quién no enhadará	

	los desvaríos que aquí van.		
PARVO.	Mirad vos quien sofrirá		65
	las mochachas que aquí están.		
	¿Haste d'ir hoy?		
FILÓSOFO.	Dexa ya essa necedá.		
PARVO.	¿Y pensáis que faltará		
	otra, mi amo garrido?		70
FILÓSOFO.	Señores, yo soy venido...		
PARVO.	Señores, ahora llegamos.		
FILÓSOFO.	¡Calla, necio dolorido!		
	¡Mejor fuera consomido		
	el día que nos juntamos!		75
PARVO.	Dezid, nuestramo, veamos:		
	¿son mejores de comer		
	las grajas o los milanos?		
	Y más ¿sabéis qué yo querría?		
	Dormir quatro o cinco meses.		80
FILÓSOFO.	Ya desseo que dormiesses,		
	porque la embaxada mía		
	no la empidan tus reveses.		
PARVO.	Pues, mi amo, echaos vos		
	y dormiremos a la una.		85
FILÓSOFO.	Menguada estava la luna,		
	quando nacimos los dos,		
	y contraria la fortuna.		
	Después dormiré yo, amigo.		
	En tanto tú dormirás		90
	y no soñarás comigo;		
	mas yo soñaré contigo		
	por quanta pena me das.		
	Porque qualquiera passión,		
	asegún veo y entiendo,	[d]	95
	que se siente con razón,		
	ni velando ni dormiendo		
	se consuela el coraçón.		
PARVO.	Pues aborrís la dormida,		
	no os vais por ahí andando;		100
	ni me llevéis arrastrando,		

nuestramo, por vuestra vida,
por vos irdes escapando.

Deita-s'o Parvo *a dormir, e diz o* Filósofo:

Veis que hago penitencia
desta suerte sin pecar; 105
y es tanta mi paciencia,
siendo tal la penitencia,
que no me quiero ausentar.
Porque la obediencia, amigo,
las virtudes son sus puentes: 110
en tu hablar no te isientes,
porque te vas del abrigo
al peligro que no sientes.
Aunque el daño sea profano,
ésta toma por tu guía, 115
que yo tengo al Coleo Romano,
aunque me fue inhumano,
obediencia todavía.
Y en quanto la compañía,
que la fortuna me dio, 120
duerme, anunciaré yo
una fiesta de alegría,
que de nuevo se inventó.
Y pues me tiene dexado,
del autor diré el intento; 125
y, por ir más declarado,
será en prosa el argumento.
Peró, señores, os pido
que tengáis todo encubierto,
en vuestro seno escondido, 130
por que no sepa Copido
que descubro su secreto.

[*fo.* 115 *r*]

La comedia seguiente, altos y famosos señores, su nombre es Floresta d'engaños. Y el primero engaño es que un pobre escudero engañó un mercader, en figura de muger beúda. El segundo engaño será que siendo Copido enamorado de la princesa Grata Celia, la qual era hija del rey Telebano, Rey de Tesalia. Por lo qual, siendo Grata Celia hija deste rey y señora de la más excelencia y estremada hermosura del mundo. No podiendo Copido haver con ella lugar solitario ni tiempo oportuno, descanso de su angustiada vida, determinó de engañar al dios Apolo, por que el dios Apolo engañasse al rey Telebano. Y el rey Telebano, engañado del dios Apolo, llevó Grata Celia engañada a la sierra Minea, adonde, con grande angustia, su padre la dexó desterrada y presa. Y quando Copido huvo alcançado y hecho su engaño, descendió del cielo a la tierra, donde presa estava, y fue della engañado dos vezes, y ella casada con el Príncipe de la Gran Grecia.

PARVO. ¿Havémonos hoy de ir? [fo. 115 a]
FILÓSOFO. Ya ha dos horas que te llamo.
PARVO. Yo os doy mi fe, nuestramo, 135
    que es gran trabajo el dormir.
FILÓSOFO. Nuestro argumento acabado,
    el mercader veréis entrar,
    y pensando d'engañar,
    ha de quedar engañado. 140

Sae-se o FILÓSOFO *e entra o* MERCADOR.

MERCADOR. Determino de fazer
    minhas casas muito bem,
    porque quem dinheiro tem
    fará tudo o que quiser.
    Bem contados 145
    tenho vinte mil cruzados,
    ganhados d'onzenas tais
    com êsses pobres misteirais
    que estávão necessitados.
     E parece-me agora [b] 150
    que vejo desta janela
    vir pera cá uma senhora;
    e, segundo o ar de fora,
    viúva me parece ela.

Môça.	Hou da pousada!	155
	Senhor, uma dona honrada	
	está aqui pera vos falar.	
Mercador.	Entre cá, s'ela mandar,	
	que eu nam faço agora nada.	
Viúva.	Olha cá, mexeriqueirinha,	160
	nam me descubras tu a mi.	
Môça.	Nam farei, por vida minha.	
Viúva.	Porque és a mor palreirinha	
	que eu em minha vida vi.	
Môça.	Que prazer!	165
	E eu havia de dizer	
	que éreis pobre escudeirão,	
	sem cavalo e sem tostão	
	e em trajos de molher,	
	que is enganar um ladrão!	170
	Guarde-me Deus! e vós nam vêdes? [c]	
	Segredo nam-no posso ter	
	se achar a quem-no dizer,	
	e senám essas paredes:	
	que o costume	175
	é tam acendido lume,	
	depois que está encarnado,	
	que, até nam ser acabado,	
	nenhuma cousa o consume.	

Diz a Viúva *ao* Mercador:

	Senhor, embora estejais.	180
Mercador.	Embora venhais, senhora;	
	que é o que demandais?	
Viúva.	Eu o direi ora:	
	Ai coitada,	
	que venho ora tam cansada	185
	do corpo e doutras canseiras!	
Mercador.	Sentai-vos nessas cadeiras.	
Viúva.	Esse descanso nam é nada.	
	Crede que a necessidade	
	mui pouco descanso tem.	190

Mercador.	Assi viva eu que é verdade,	
	e falastes muito bem,	
	muito à minha vontade.	
Viúva.	Digo, senhor,	
	que o tisoureiro-mor,	195
	do nobre Rei Telebano,	
	me deve já do outro ano	
	as tenças de meu suor.	
Môça (*aside*).	Tens tu lá tenças de vento.	
Mercador.	O dinheiro quanto é?	200
Viúva.	Êste papel dará fé,	
	que é o seu conhecimento.	
Mercador.	Mostrai cá, verei que é.	
	Bem estaes:	
	sam corenta mil reaes.	205
Viúva.	Senhor, eu estou enforcada,	
	e se vós nam mos comprais,	
	à menhám sam penhorada.	
Mercador.	Nam me faleis nisso mais; [*d*]	
	nam farei eu tal, por certo.	210
Viúva.	Nam é essa boa reposta.	
Mercador.	E a pena que está posta?	
Viúva.	Será secreto o concêrto.	
Mercador.	Nam pode ser.	
Viúva.	Quem há isso de saber?	215
Mercador.	Quando os fôr arrecadar.	
Viúva.	Nam me queirais desconsolar.	
	Vós o sabereis fazer.	
Mercador.	Ora, em fim, quero ser tolo sandeu,	
	e só por vos socorrer.	220
	Quanto mos quereis vender?	
Viúva.	Em vossa alma o deixo eu.	
Mercador.	Eu vos direi:	
	dez mil reaes vos darei:	
	êstes logo em bos tostões.	225
Viúva.	Ai Jesu, aque-del-Rei!	
Mercador.	Eu daqui nam passarei,	
	nem passemos mais rezões.	
Viúva.	A uma viúva amara	

	fazeis tamanha crueza?	230
	Oh coitada da pobreza	
	que tudo a desempara!	
Mercador.	No-mais, senhora.	
Viúva.	Nam vos contentareis ora	
	com vinte mil, que é a metade?	235
Mercador.	Nem com mais cinco, em verdade.	
Viúva.	Dai-mos já com a má-hora.	

Despois da Viúva *receber o dinheiro, vai-se dizendo:*

        Nam havia em Portugal,
        nos tempos mais ancianos,
        tantas maneiras d'enganos,   240
        nem tantos males dum mal.
Mercador. Vá-se embora,
        que trinta mil deixa a senhora
        nêste desembargo seu;
        porém nam-na esfolara eu   245
        s'ela doutra casta fôra.

Vem a Môça *que veo com a* Viúva *e diz:*   [*fo.* 116 *a*]

        Mercador, quereis saber?
        Bem enganado ficastes,
        que a viúva que enganastes
        era homem e não molher.   250
        E mais, é vento
        êsse seu conhecimento;
        êle o assinou e nam mais.
        Assi que os dez mil reais
        leixai-os no testamento.   255
Mercador. Crede que quem fôr tirano,
        tem seu dinheiro perdido.
        Vamo-nos, que vem Copido
        cometer o mor engano
        que nunca foi cometido;   260
        em o qual
        mostra o amor natural

que a Grata Célia tem,
porém vereis que do bem
às vezes se segue mal. 265

Vem COPIDO *e diz*:

¿A quién contaré mis quexas,
a quién diré mi tormento?
¿Remedio, por qué te alexas
de ver Amor que solo dexas
neste término momento? 270
Oh justa esperança mía,
¿qué fue de mí y de ti?
Si te viesse algún día,
ya no te conocería;
tanto ha que no te vi. 275
Los que me pintan ciego,
no es ansí como conviene;
que Amor tantos ojos tiene
como de muertes me ruego,
y ninguna me conviene. 280
¡Oh Grata Celia, alma mía,
flor del más florido huerto!
Pues que a tu Dios tienes muerto,
arrepiéndete algún día [b]
de tan grande desconcierto. 285
Hiere tu pecho honrado
sobre el bravo coraçón;
contemplando en mi passión
verás que en el fuego en que ardo
me echaste sin razón. 290
Oh ingrata pecador,
rasga el coraçón esquivo,
que mataste al dios d'amor.
Y para más mi dolor,
me dexaste el amor bivo. 295
Si aquesto no conocieres,
más penitencia no hagas;
que bien sé el mal que me quieres,

	y los gozos y plazeres	
	que recibes con mis llagas.	300
	Penitencia será harta	
	pensares en mi tormento,	
	sólo por el merecimiento,	
	que al complir de mi carta	
	hize en mí tu pensamiento.	305
	Grata Celia es muy guardada	
	en sus palacios reales,	
	de su padre muy amada;	
	y ella, no se le da nada	
	de mis dolorosos males.	310
	Dios Apolo vendrá ora.	
	Cúmpleme de usar engaño,	
	que el engaño no es estraño;	
	antes se usa cada hora,	
	y la verdad d'año en año.	315

Chega Apolo *e diz*:

	Norabuena estéis, Copido.	
Cupido.	Apolo, seas loado.	
Apolo.	Señor, ¿eres namorado?	
Cupido.	Antes traigo mi sentido	
	bien fuera desse cuidado.	320
Apolo.	Pues ¿qué hazes por aquí,	
	por esta floresta d'engaños? [c]	
Cupido.	Ando esperando por ti.	
Apolo.	¿Qué es lo que quieres de mí?	
Cupido.	Que bivas cuento de años.	325
	El Rey Telebano	
	es tu devoto y grande amigo;	
	bien en secreto te digo	
	que, antes que passe un año,	
	terná peligro consigo;	330
	y el tu templo corre risco,	
	porque esta ciudad será	
	toda assolada a barrisco.	
Apolo.	Esso ¿qué lo causará?	

Cupido.	Tiene hecho tantos males	335

Cupido.   Tiene hecho tantos males   335
          Grata Celia, de secreto,
          a las diosas divinales,
          pecados tan criminales,
          que lo que digo es cierto.
Apolo.   ¿Puédese remediar?   340
Cupido.   El remedio está en la mano
          si hiziere el Rey Telebano,
          por tanto mal escusar,
          lo que te diré, hermano.
              Lleve su hija daquí   345
          a aquella serra Minea,
          adonde sin ella se vea,
          y haga penitencia allí
          por que perdonada sea.
Apolo.   Caro le será de obrar.   350
Cupido.   Más caro es perder su estado,
          la vida y el reinar,
          y la Reina y su mandar,
          y el pueblo ser ablasado.
              Y Grata Celia escondida,   355
          allí sola, desterrada,
          salvará también su vida;
          pues que siendo oferecida,
          será libre y perdonada.
Apolo.   Yo lo haré en verdad   360
          por se escusar tanta muerte.
Cupido.   Apolo, haze de suerte   [d]
          que restaures la ciudad,
          que el peligro es muy fuerte.
              Tú has se lo de mandar,   365
          que aquí no cabe ruego;
          porque él lo hará luego,
          aunque será con pesar,
          por escusar mayor fuego.
Apolo.   Luego voy adó está   370
          o él vendrá adó estó.
Cupido.   Entremetes yo me vo,
          que todo se amansará

con esto que digo yo.
    Yo bien sé que erro ahora, 375
mas es por sanar un daño.
Perdóname, mi señora,
que el mundo triste dagora
se llama templo d'engaño.
    Ya el Rey Telebano está 380
delante de Apolo rezando.
Veamos cómo saldrá
o quándo se cumplirá
lo que yo estoy deseando.

Vai el Rei Telebano *fazer oração ao deos* Apolo, *e diz* Apolo:

    Vuestra Alteza reze breve 385
y obre obras de sancto,
que el rezar no monta tanto
como hazer lo que se deve.
El rezar es como flores
y flores las oraciones, 390
y el fructo, dizen doctores,
las obras son los amores,
y no las buenas razones.
    Tenemos mucho que hablar,
y vos mucho que hazer: 395
cosas de vuestro pesar.
Y havéis de perdonar,
pues no se puede escusar,
ni menos no puede ser.
Vuestro reino está en peligro 400
y mi templo amenazado,
vuestro palacio juzgado
de las diosas deste siglo,   [*fo.* 117 *a*]
que será todo assolado.
    Y porque es longo de dezir 405
las cosas que esto hizieron,
yo las quiero resomir;
pero havéis de sentir
que de vuestra casa nacieron.

	Solíamos en la paz estar	410
	de Verecinta, Julia y Palas;	
	ahora están con tan ferozes alas	
	que no quieren escuchar	
	razones buenas ni malas.	
TELEBANO.	Oh muy precioso Apolo,	415
	pues siempre serví a vos,	
	ahora es tiempo, mi Dios,	
	mi amparo y mi consuelo,	
	que os acordéis de nos.	
APOLO.	Son diesas muy furiosas:	420
	ya sabéis que las mugeres,	
	quando están más amorosas,	
	más blandas, más piadosas,	
	no son menos que crueles;	
	¿qué harán siendo sañosas?	425
	Que sólo un remedio tenéis,	
	aunque muy caro os sea:	
	Grata Celia llevaréis	
	a aquella sierra Minea	
	y presa la dexaréis.	430
	Y llevalda por engaño,	
	por la floresta d'engaños,	
	a la sierra, adó en dos años	
	vos librará deste daño.	
TELEBANO.	¿En perder mi hija gano?	435
APOLO.	Sí: el reino y la ciudad,	
	templo y conmunidad;	
	catad que os será muy sano.	
	Y, por el mal no ser nada,	
	os mando que lo hagáis.	440
TELEBANO.	Pues, Señor, vos lo mandáis,	
	Grata Celia desdichada [b]	
	irá onde la ordenáis.	

Vai-se APOLO, *e fica el Rei* TELEBANO *dizendo*:

¡Oh graves angustias mías,
lágrimas dell ánima mía!   445

¡Oh hija de mi alegría!
¿Qué tales serán mis días
fuera de tu compañía?
Quedarás en las montañas,
naquella Minea sierra, 450
y mis beços y mis canas
mucho en breve serán tierra.

Chega a Princesa GRATA CÉLIA *e diz*:

           Señor mío, ¿por qué andáis
pensativo y amarillo?
Muy mucho me maravillo: 455
¿qué sentís o qué pensáis?

TELEBANO. Es passión.
GRATA. No sé qué lágrimas son
essas que veo assomar;
algún estremo pesar 460
siente vuesso coraçón.
    Yo contemplo ciertamente
que caros son los enojos
que se estilan por los ojos
de un Rey tan sabio y prudente. 465
Padre, vos
no os congoxéis, por Dios,
que el enojo muerte ordena.
TELEBANO. Por quitar de mí esta pena,
vamos a caçar los dos. 470
GRATA. Señor, vamos norabuena.

Entra um DOCTOR, *Justiça Maior do reino, e diz o* REI:

           Doctor muy sabio, prudente,
pues sois Justicia Mayor, [c]
hazeldo despachadamente,
con tal zelo y hervor 475
como se yo fuesse presente.
    Voy en una romería
con Grata Celia y no más;

	hazed que no buelva atrás	
	la justicia que solía	480
	ser igual.	
	Por cierto, el mayor mal	
	y que en mi reino más importa	
	es la justicia estar muerta,	
	y el derecho mortal,	485
	y la cobdicia despierta.	
	Buen letrado sin desvío	
	sois y siempre cuerdo os vi.	
DOCTOR.	Señor, yo lo haré ansí	
	porque lo tengo de mío.	490
TELEBANO.	Hija, vamos;	
	veremos aquí los engaños	
	y quiçá me alegraré.	
GRATA.	Padre, yo no sé qué he,	
	porque, quanto más andamos,	495
	voy triste y no sé por qué.	

Ido el Rei TELEBANO *com sua filha, abre o* DOCTOR *um livro de leis e diz, lendo por êle*:

"*Princeps osivi me nova per delegantem, per novaciones antiquaque.*"

E estando o DOCTOR *assi estudando, veo uma* MÔÇA *ter com êle, à qual êle diz*:

	¿Qué buscaes acá, señora?	
MÔÇA.	Senhor, vinha-vos falar.	
DOCTOR.	Y pues ¿no havéis d'entrar?	
MÔÇA.	Entrarei, mas nam jagora.	500
DOCTOR.	Y pues ¿quándo?	
MÔÇA.	Estais agora estudando	
	só, e eu sam grande já.	[d]
DOCTOR.	No sé qué estáis recelando.	
MÔÇA.	Mas será bem que me vá.	505
DOCTOR.	Si traéis, hija, algún pleito,	
	¿queréis consejo de mí?	
MÔÇA.	A isso vinha eu aqui,	

	por ver se tenho dereito.	
Doctor.	Si es a esso,	510
	recontadme el hecho vuesso	
	y entrad bien sin temor.	
Môça.	Sabeis quê, senhor Doctor?	
	Vós pareceis-me travêsso.	
Doctor.	Ya hize sessenta y seis,	515
	ya mi tiempo es passado.	
Môça.	Nam sei que anos havés,	
	mas olhais-me de través	
	e com o barrete embicado.	
	E por isso	520
	me quero acolher ao siso.	
Doctor.	¡Oh, entrad acá, señora,	
	mi sagrado paraíso!	
Môça.	Já disse que nam jagora;	
	logo assi tam improviso?	525
	E mais, vós falais-me amores,	
	e nam já ora muito frios.	
Doctor.	Pues ¿qué haré yo, mis flores,	
	a los ojos matadores	
	que me cegaron los míos?	530
Môça.	Quem tal quer	
	nam havia de ter molher,	
	e fermosa como a vossa.	
Doctor.	¡Oh mi perla preciosa!	
	No me hagáis entender	535
	que sin vos haya hermosa.	
Môça.	Dai-me conselho, vos digo,	
	numa demanda que trago.	
Doctor.	¿E qué me daréis en pago?	
Môça.	E tanto sois meu amigo?	540
Doctor.	Yo no quiero	
	de vos plata ni dinero, [fo. 118 a]	
	mas privar con vos por cierto	
	en lugar mucho secreto,	
	por deziros quánto os quiero.	545
	Yo daré, juro a Dios,	
	la sentencia en vuesso hecho;	

	y aunque no tengáis derecho	
	todo ello saldrá por vos,	
	y haréis vuesso provecho.	550
Môça.	Muitembora.	
	Senhor, minha dona agora	
	vai-se mui cedo deitar,	
	e esta noite hei d'amassar	
	e bem sabeis onde mora.	555

      Ide antre as nove e as dez—
assoviaes vós bem, meu rei?
Ou tossi tamalaves
que logo vos entenderei.
E eu me vou   560
que há já muito que cá estou.

Doctor.   Y yo también me vo a jantar.
Môça.   Oh, como hei d'enganar
um doutor que se enganou!

      Alguidar, ora vem cá,   565
e faremos o formento;
que negro contentamento
o negro doutor terá,
do que lh'há de sair vento.

      Canta a Môça:

"Enganado andais, amigo,   570
dias há que vo-lo digo."

Assovia o Doutor *à porta da* Môça, *e ela diz*:

      Olhai-me aquêle assoviar!
Como vai lindo e secreto!
Aquêle dissimular!
Crede que mao é d'achar   575
um letrado ser discreto.

      (*Vai-lhe abrir*)

Senhor Doutor,
verdadeiro é vosso amor,   [*b*]

	pois vos traz per tal caminho.
	Sobireis muito passinho, 580
	e vinde por onde eu fôr.
	Entrai vós e a vara nam,
	que nam quero que cá prenda.
Doctor.	Sí, que es vara de condón
	que me da gruessa hazienda; 585
	y, aunque ella poco me rienda,
	dame mucha ocasión.
Môça.	Nam tussais má-hora agora.
Doctor.	¿Aquí amassáis, señora?
Môça.	Senhor, si...
Doctor.	Y ¿adónde dormís? 590
Môça.	Falai vós passinho, ouvis?

ou vos tornai pera fora.
   Tirai a loba e dai-ma cá;
luvas, e sombreiro, e tudo,
e a beca de veludo, 595
que tudo se guardará.
E entám fazeis-vos mudo;
item mais:
guardai-vos que nam tussais,
e vesti esta fraldilha, 600
e ponde esta beatilha,
e fazei que peneirais.

Peneira o Doutor, *e diz a* Môça:

Nam peneirais bem, Doutor;
quero-vos dar uma liçám:
tomai aqui com esta mão, 605
ora andai assi ao redor...
ah! isso vai muito loução.
Eu quero ir ver que faz
minha dona; entám veremos,
porque em tudo o que fazemos 610
há mister manhas assaz
segundo o mundo que temos.

Doctor.	¿Y si ella dallá me ve?		
Môça.	Direi que a negra peneira;		
	e em quanto ela joeira,	[c]	615
	peneire vossa mercê.		
Doctor.	Paciencia;		
	porque juro en mi conciencia		
	que este texto yo no lo entiendo.		
	Peró si yo estoy cirniendo,		620
	es en loor y reverencia		
	del amor a que me riendo.		
	Estas bueltas no sé yo.		
	Dulcis amor, qui me vis?		
	Que no se aprende en París		625
	este lavor en que estó.		
	¡Oh amor!		
Môça.	Peneirai, senhor Doutor,		
	asinha que vem minha dona.		
Doctor.	¡Oh de las lindas coronas,		630
	amad a tal servidor!		
Môça.	Nam vêdes, dona, esta perra		
	o negro geito que tem?		
Velha.	Peneirai, má-hora, bem,		
	que nam sois nova na terra.		635
	Hui, cadelinha,		
	onde geitas a farinha?		
	Nam queres falar, cadela?		
	Esta pele de toninha		
	olho mao se meteo nela.		640
Doctor.	¿Por qué vos, mía señora,		
	estar tanto destemplado?		
	Ya tudo estar peneirada.		
	¿Qué bradar comigo ahora?		
	¿Qué cousa estar vos hablanda?		645
	A mí llamá Caterina Furnando,		
	nunca a mí cadela nam.		
Velha.	S'eu dali tomo um tiçám...		
	e vós, estais patorneando?		
	Olhade a mal entrouxada!		650
	Oh almadraque bolorento!		

Môça.	Hui, faze asinha o formento e amassarás de madrugada: estará o forno milhor.		
Velha.	E que é daquêle doutor que dizes que tens aqui?	[d]	655
Môça.	Perto está êle de mi, e eu longe do seu amor.		
Velha.	Está escondido? Mostra-m'êsse homem perdido.		660
Môça.	Hi está êle a peneirar, e êle mesmo há d'amassar, porque a negra é co marido.		
Velha.	E negro falam os doutores? Nunca eu vi taes diferenças.		665
Môça.	Pois que hi há negras sentenças, nam haverá hi alguns negros ouvidores em algumas audiências?		
Velha.	Que canseira!		
Môça.	Eu o pus dessa maneira porque me falou d'amor.		670
Velha.	Jesu! e quem vio doutor em fraldas de panadeira? Dizede, Doutor da má-hora, e falai-me per latim: que diz o Bártolo aqui?		675
Doctor.	No so yo solo, señora, que otros muchos huvo ahí y micelos.		
Velha.	Havíeis mister farelos ou que peneirada é essa?		680
Doctor.	Vuestra nieta es muy traviessa.		
Velha.	Hei-vos de ver os cabelos. Dai-me cá êsse toucado... Olhade aquela honestidade! Um doutor daquela idade andar tam desarranjado, em tal maneira!		685
Doctor.	¿Ónde porné la penera?		
Velha.	Que má-hora cá tornastes,		690

que tam tarde começastes
a ser doutor e pàdeira.
　No Baldo acharíeis, Doutor,
essa negra amassadura　　[fo. 119 a]
ou na sagrada Escretura?　　　　　　695
Dize Bucodonosor
que essas cans
tornarám-se canas vans.
Jesu, que mao estudar,
e que má livro é o alguidar,　　　　　700
e que letras ancians!
　E môça queríeis vós?
E *per quam regula*, micer,
cuidou vosso parecer
que já a tínheis nas piós?　　　　　　705
Mana minha!
E nam abasta a farinha
que fazedes no julgar,
senám virdes peneirar
uma pouca que aqui tinha,　　　　　710
no fundo do alguidar?

MÔÇA.　　Bem vos diz essa fraldilha;
quereis vós bailar comigo?
DOCTOR.　Que haga esto el enemigo
no es mucha maravilla,　　　　　　715
según es.
MÔÇA.　　Sabeis que me pareceis?
Ermitám que endoudeceo;
milhor vos estava o veo
que quanto en casa trazeis.　　　　　720
　Dona, dona, vai fogindo.
VELHA.　Vá-se muitieramá.
MÔÇA.　　A loba lhe fica cá.
Oh, como vai tam corrido!

　Torna o DOUTOR *e diz*:

　Acá me ha quedado todo:　　　　　725
una beca de veludo

	y loba de contray frisado,	
	que se me quedó olvidado.	
	No vaya todo tan crudo.	
Môça.	E vós, Doutor, ervilhastes?	730
	Vindes vós em vosso siso? [b]	
	Que mentira!	
	Ide prègar Altemira,	
	que s'eu quisesse falar...	
	Mais quiséreis vós furtar	735
	se vo-lo eu consentira.	
Doctor.	¿Quién pensara norabuena	
	que una rapaza de un año	
	hiziera tan grande engaño	
	a un doctor hecho en Sena?	740
	Será más sano	
	callar hecho tan profano	
	y olvidar esta guerra,	
	y irme a juzgar la tierra,	
	que ya el Rey Telebano	745
	ahora llega a la sierra.	

Aqui se representa o que passou el Rei Telebano *na serra Minèa com* Grata Célia, *sua filha.*

Telebano.	Grata Celia, hija mía,	
	ésta es la sierra Minea,	
	la qual vuestra casa sea	
	de lágrimas sin alegría.	750
Grata.	¿Por qué, señor?	
Telebano.	Porque yo, por mi dolor,	
	os he traída engañada,	
	de mi casa desterrada.	
Grata.	¿Por qué, triste pecador?	755
	Que yo no os hize nada.	
Telebano.	Mándalo Apolo Dios,	
	y me metió neste afán;	
	y, como hizo Abrahán,	
	hago sacreficio de vos.	760
Grata.	¡Oh triste yo!	

     Ya sé quién esto ordenó:
     Copido hizo estos daños.
     ¡Oh mis tristes quinze años!
     Mal haya quien los mató.   765
TELEBANO. Perdonáme, hija, vos   [c]
     que havéis de quedar presa
     en medio desta defesa,
     porque ansí lo manda Dios.
GRATA.   ¡Oh perdida!   770
     Saquéisme, padre, la vida
     de que fuistes causador.
     Quel morir no es dolor;
     más dolor es la guarida.
     Perded manzilla de mí   775
     y matadme, señor padre,
     que saludad de mi madre
     me mata ansí como ansí.
TELEBANO. ¿Matar?
     Aún Dios tiene que dar.   780
     Esfuerce vuestro dolor,
     que vuestra dicha mayor
     por aquí la havéis d'hallar.
GRATA.   ¿Qué dicha puedo yo topar
     fuera de vuestro poder?   785
TELEBANO. Hija, yo os verné a ver
     quando lo Apolo mandar.

    Vai-se el REI, *e diz* GRATA CÉLIA:

     Grata Celia, ¿qué es de ti
     y del vicio que tenías?
     Que las noches y los días   790
     eran todos pera mí.
     ¿Quién traxo Copido aquí
     a escuchar las ansias mías?
CUPIDO.   Pues sois remedio del daño
     que consume mis plazeres,   795
     bendito seas engaño
     que, con tu poder estraño,

	todo acabas quanto quieres.	
	En ti mora	
	todo el descanso dahora:	800
	tú lo das, por ti se da.	
	Mi vida te la dará,	
	pues me la diste, señora.	
	Prefeción de las mugeres, [d]	
	vos me quitastes la vida	805
	y la tenéis consumida,	
	y mis bienes y plazeres.	
	Y viéndoos puesta	
	en esta brava floresta	
	y entre estas espessuras,	810
	dexé el cielo a escuras	
	por ver la claridá vuestra.	
	No por sanar mi passión	
	ni menguar en mis enojos,	
	porque vuessos rayos son	815
	dolores al coraçón	
	y lágrimas a los ojos.	
Grata.	Podéis hablar,	
	que yo tengo d'escuchar;	
	pues, triste por mi dolor,	820
	Telebano, mi señor,	
	me dexó neste lugar	
	ansí como me hallastes,	
	presa nestos fierros tristes.	
Cupido.	Quántas vezes me matastes,	825
	y quántas me despreciastes	
	hasta que me despedistes.	
	Pues ahora,	
	oh Princesa, mi señora,	
	cesse vuessa señoría,	830
	porque el dios que se enamora,	
	si lo adoran, él os adora,	
	y siempre os adoraría.	
	Dadme vuesso amor real,	
	que realmente os serví.	835
Grata.	¿Qué amor queréis de mí?	

| | Yo misma me quiero mal
y al día en que nascí.
Y ¿qué hize, triste yo,
que tanto mal me hizieron?   840
¿Qué pecado me prendió?
¿Qué culpa me desterró?
¿Por qué tal pena me dieron? |
| --- | --- |
| CUPIDO. | Señora, cessen por Dios   [fo. 120 a]
vuestras quexas y renzillas,   845
que, pues yo muero por vos,
escusadas son dezillas.
Amor os pido. |
| GRATA. | Pues vos sois el dios Copido,
que todo amor tiene en sí,   850
¿qué amor pedís a mí? |
| CUPIDO. | Mas ¿qué ganáis vos aquí
en traer un dios perdido? |
| GRATA. | Si amor de mí queréis,
aquí está esta cadena: 855
si con ella vos prendéis,
señor, vos me cobraréis
y os sacaré de pena
nesta hora. |
| CUPIDO. | Que me plaze, mi señora.   860
Vuesso cautivo me quiero,
y de vuestra alteza espero
cumplir lo que dixe ahora. |

Tira COPIDO *a prisám a* GRATA CÉLIA, *e ela prende a éle,
e diz* COPIDO:

| | ¡Oh qué prisiones tan tristes
son las vuessas, mi señora!   865 |
| --- | --- |
| GRATA. | ¡Ah! yo me vengaré ahora
del mal que vos me hezistes.
Que si fuera
vuesso amor de tal manera
como dais a presumir,   870 |

	escogiérades morir		
	antes que tal me hiziera.		
	Fue una cruda hazaña		
	que hizo el cruel traidor;		
	porque el verdadero amor		875
	a nadia jamás engaña.		
CUPIDO.	Vuestro so,		
	y si no os tuviera yo		
	amor en tanta manera,		
	del cielo no descendiera	[b]	880
	al gran peligro en que estó.		
	¡Oh celeste hermosura!		
	Vos me queráis perdonar,		
	que para poderos hablar		
	me puse en tanta ventura		885
	y a vos en tanto pesar.		
GRATA.	¿No os dolían		
	lágrimas que me corrían,		
	que cada hora era un río?		
CUPIDO.	Señora mía, yo os fío		890
	que todas ellas salían		
	del triste coraçón mío.		
GRATA.	Ora, cred aquello vos		
	y veréis qué os saldrá:		
	el diablo conocerá		895
	raposo en traje de Dios.		
	Quedaos ahí,		
	que yo me voy por aquí		
	a oír los ruisinoles.		
	No quiero escuchar amores,		900
	pues nunca los conocí.		
	Bendita sea la muger		
	que de los hombres no fía,		
	y maldita la que confía		
	en su dañoso querer;		905
	y bendita		
	toda muger que se quita		
	de oír sus dulces engaños,		

que doblados son los daños
que dello se remerita. 910
   Como río furioso
son los hombres, sin descanso;
porque adó corre más manso,
allí está más peligroso,
porque es hondo aquel remanso. 915
Y según huelo,
son como sotil anzuelo
quando se viste d'engaño;
que en todo el tiempo del año   [c]
de fuera muestra consuelo, 920
y de dentro tiene engaño.

CUPIDO.   Reñiego de la venida,
pues doblados son mis daños.
¡Oh, quántos modos d'engaños
ha hí en esta triste vida! 925
Que ansí acaeció
que Apolo la engañó,
y fue por industria mía;
mas el amor que le tenía
tuvo la culpa y no yo. 930
   ¡Oh mugeres, oh mugeres!
Robadoras de las vidas,
crueles, desconocidas,
destruición de plazeres.
Coriosas, 935
ufanas, desamorosas,
autorizadas, movibles,
y de todo envejosas,
que tienen cosas terribles.

Vem um PASTOR *rústico e diz:*

   Ora eu estou espantado. 940
Sendo vós Sam Sodorninho,
como errastes o caminho
lá abaixo a par do valado?
Ou m'engano?

Cupido.	Allégate acá, hermano.	945
Pastor.	Ora m'enganava tanto	
	que cuidei que éreis vós santo,	
	e vós falais castelhano.	
	Pois, que estais aqui fazendo?	
Cupido.	¿Qués que te lo haga saber?	950
	Tú no lo has d'entender,	
	que yo mismo no lo entiendo	
	por ahora.	
Pastor.	E vós estais preso, má-hora?	
Cupido.	Pastor, esto no es prisión,	955
	que es cadena de condón, [d]	
	que me dio una señora	
	de mucha veneración.	
	El que en ella se prendiere	
	será libre de tristeza,	960
	y mil bienes y riqueza	
	terná quien nella estuviere,	
	por mi fe.	
	Y pues tu ventura fue	
	que tú alcançasses vella,	965
	yo te hago merced della	
	y Dios te hará mercé;	
	gózate mucho en tenella.	
	Quítamela con tu mano.	
Pastor.	Esta veo do Perú.	970
	Ora Deus me trouxe aqui.	
Cupido.	Dala acá, ponla en ti:	
	buena prol te haga, hermano.	
Pastor.	Oh coitado!	
Cupido.	¿Qué has?	
Pastor.	Estou namorado.	975
Cupido.	¿De quién?	
Pastor.	Que sei eu de quem,	
	senám que o amor me tem	
	o coraçám apertado?	
	E segundo a fortaleza	
	com que m'aperta e namora,	980
	deve ser a mor senhora	

                    que se criou em Veneza.
                    Cego sou
                    e nam sei quem me cegou,
                    por nam ter cura meu mal.　　　　985
                    Bofá, vós sois um enxoval;
                    mas quem em vós se fiou
                    merece ter pago tal.
CUPIDO.　　　　Se desta pena te sacas,
　　　　　　　tu bivir muy mal s'emplea.　　　　990
PASTOR.　　　Oh, tirai-me esta cadea
　　　　　　　que se me perdem as vacas
　　　　　　　sem pastor.
　　　　　　　E sòmente o amor
　　　　　　　nos mata de uma pastôra.　　　　995
　　　　　　　Se fôra dest'outra dor...　　[fo. 121 a]
　　　　　　　Oh, pesar de vós, Amor,
　　　　　　　que o diabo vos trouxe ora!
CUPIDO.　　　　Mueres d'amores, hermano.
PASTOR.　　　Em mi tal amor que monta?　　　　1000
　　　　　　　E pois foi êrro de conta.
　　　　　　　desfaçamo-lo engano.
　　　　　　　Ora ouvi.
CUPIDO.　　　Es ésta que vene aquí.
PASTOR.　　　Pardeos! Esta vos é ela!　　　　1005
　　　　　　　Ora olhai, corpo de mim,
　　　　　　　que presta a um vilám roim
　　　　　　　ir amar tam alta estrêla?
　　　　　　　Eu sam indino pastor,
　　　　　　　pobre, vestido de pele;　　　　1010
　　　　　　　de ser preso em vosso amor
　　　　　　　enganou-me êste senhor,
　　　　　　　que má viagem faça êle.
　　　　　　　Que m'olhais?
　　　　　　　Um fraco pastor matais　　　　1015
　　　　　　　e nam é cousa honesta;
　　　　　　　que a cárrega que lançais
　　　　　　　à mula que carregais
　　　　　　　pesa muito mais que a bêsta.

GRATA.	¿No os digo, Dios d'amor,	1020
	que no es nada el vuestro amar?	
	Que para os esprementar	
	os hize aquel disfavor,	
	y no para os olvidar.	
	Por mi vida,	1025
	que ahora a esso venía,	
	y hállovos sin prisión,	
	sin congoxa y sin passión;	
	no pidáis más alegría.	
CUPIDO.	Vuestras crueles renzillas	1030
	y grandes desesperanças	
	y tan bravas esquivanças	
	hazen estas maravillas.	
	Y no sé qué más os diga. [b]	
PASTOR.	Fazei uma cousa boa:	1035
	eu nam sam aqui pessoa;	
	soltar-me desta fadiga	
	por vossa vida, senhora.	
GRATA.	Poco ha que dixistes vos	
	de las mugeres mil males:	1040
	que eran crudas, desleales,	
	y otras mil plagas de nos.	
	Y vos, Amor,	
	deviérades sentir mejor,	
	que no son nada las faltas	1045
	para las virtudes altas,	
	que les dan mucho loor.	
CUPIDO.	Esso dixo mi passión,	
	porque, quando ella no mengua,	
	haze dezir a la lengua	1050
	lo que niega el coraçón.	
	Es tan llano	
	las mugeres a una mano	
	ser la prefeción del mundo,	
	en la tierra el soberano,	1055
	en el cielo el bien segundo.	
GRATA.	Copido, pues estáis fuera,	
	prendéos en mi prisión,	

porque el alto galardón
no se gana en media hora. 1060
Ni es razón
que estea en vuestra prisión
esse rústico pastor.
Quitaldo dessa passión
y prendé a vos, Amor. 1065

CUPIDO. Ansí lo quiero hazer,
aunque por muy cierto hallo
que del amor y querer
el dulçor es de temer,
que lo ál basta llorallo. [c] 1070
Ya vé ahora
que preso estoy, mi señora.
¡Oh favor, oh favor,
quién te cobrasse algún hora!
Porque el mal que no mejora 1075
va de peor en peor.

GRATA. ¿Favor queréis? Esperad,
sossegá, que no se haze ansí.

CUPIDO. Haved manzilla de mí,
por la vuestra piedad. 1080
Que la sciencia
de mi penosa paciencia
es aguijar mis plazeres;
dadme hermosa penitencia
y usad en todo clemencia, 1085
corona de las mugeres.

Vem o DUQUE *pelegrino e diz:*

Muchas cosas de no crer
hallo por esta floresta,
mas maravilla como ésta
no se vio ni se ha de ver. 1090
Esto es cierto.
Y ¿quién traxo a este desierto
ansí sola una donzella,
por sierra tan sin concierto,

	y el Amor preso por ella?	1095
CUPIDO.	No soy preso, mas soy muerto.	
GRATA.	¿Dónde camináis acá?	
DUQUE.	Señora, voy pelegrino	
	a un templo que acá está,	
	y a él es mi camino	1100
	en compañía	
	del hijo del Rey de Hungría	
	y Príncipe de la Gran Grecia,	
	y el Cónsul de Venecia	
	de alta genelosía.	1105
	Cinco duques pelegrinos,	
	y él también pelegrino,	
	caminando sin camino [d]	
	y dexando los caminos.	
GRATA.	¿Por qué vía	1110
	hizo él su romería	
	por tan áspera montina?	
DUQUE.	Porque lleva en compañía	
	la Ventura pelegrina,	
	que lo manda y lo guía.	1115
GRATA.	Es la mi vida tan fea,	
	y mi destierro tan feo,	
	y tan cuitada me veo	
	que no quiero	
	que el que me vido me vea.	1120
CUPIDO.	¡Oh, Princesa,	
	lémbreos mi ánima presa!	
DUQUE.	¿Y princesa es ella, hermano?	
CUPIDO.	Hija del Rey Telebano	
	y de los príncipes diesa.	1125
DUQUE.	No os vais daquí, por Dios,	
	ni os escondáis, señora,	
	porque yo sé que en buen hora	
	lo veréis y él a vos.	
	¡Dichoso hado!	1130
	Él es príncipe jurado	
	y vos princesa jurada.	
	Seréis bien aventurada	

| | y él bien aventurado,
            y bendita tal jornada.   1135
            Quiérole ir descobrir
            misterio de tanto peso.
| Cupido. | Señora, y este vuestro preso
            ¿sin remedio ha de morir?
| Grata. | Y ¿por qué?   1140
            Que amor que no tiene fe
            no puede morir d'amores.
| Cupido. | ¿Por qué no creis mis dolores,
            que mi mal claro se ve?

Vem o Príncipe *de Grécia, com os cinquo* Duques *e* Senhores *pelegrinos e a* Ventura *pelegrina, cantando todos esta cantiga:*

"Muéstranos por Dios, Ventura, [*fo.* 122 *a*] 1145
en esta sierra tan bella
las venturas que hay en ella."

E, acabando de cantar, diz a Ventura:

| | Oh Grata Celia Princesa,
            de las princesas mayor,
            ¿qué os hizo el Dios d'amor   1150
            que tenéis su vida presa?
| Grata. | Más holgara
            que Ventura preguntara,
            pues que ya me conocía,
            quien me robó el alegría   1155
            y las flores de mi cara.
| Ventura. | Perdoná que perdí el norte.
| Grata. | Oh Ventura consagrada,
            que siendo de mí adorada,
            vos me distes por mi suerte   1160
            ventura desventurada.
            ¿Tal ha de ser
            por ser buena la muger,
            virtuosa sin mudança?
            ¿Dios de amor ha de querer   1165
            tomar tan cruda vengança?

Príncipe	¿De quién os quexáis, os pido,	
	Princesa de hermosura?	
Grata.	Quéxome de la Ventura	
	y de Apolo y de Cupido.	1170
Ventura.	No es cordura	
	quexaros de la Ventura.	
	Con Apolo esta demanda,	
	que naquello que Dios manda	
	no erró nada la Ventura.	1175
Príncipe.	Si vos nada aprovecháis,	
	¿para qué os llevo por guía?	
Ventura.	Yo os guío por la vía	
	que Dios quiere que vayáis.	
	Pongo figura:	1180
	dize qualquier criatura—	
	esto bien lo sabéis vos—	
	"quizo Dios y la Ventura."	
	Primero se nombra Dios, [*b*]	
	porque es cosa más segura.	1185
	Yo os guío por acá,	
	por muy venturosa vía,	
	por dar nueva alegría	
	a la reina que aquí está.	
	De manera	1190
	que ella es principal heredera	
	en la gran Persia Mayor,	
	y vos, muy alto señor,	
	no la neguéis de pracera.	
Príncipe.	Si a la princesa aplaze,	1195
	yo lo doy por otorgado,	
	pues Dios tiene limitado	
	todo aquello que se haze.	
Grata.	Contenta so;	
	mas sin padre ¿qué haré yo?	1200
	Que aunque siento mi daño,	
	la culpa tiene el engaño	
	mas el engañado no.	
Ventura.	Catá que os viene Dios a ver.	
	Princesa muy soberana,	1205

no os devéis de torcer,
que lo que se puede hoy hazer
no quede para mañana.
No esperéis más recado,
pues os es honra y provecho;   1210
quel casamiento alongado
pocas vezes se vio hecho.

A Ventura *tomou as mãos ao* Príncipe *e* Princesa, *e com sua música se acabou esta comédia, que é a derradeira dêste Segundo Livro, e a derradeira que fêz Gil Vicente em seus dias.*

NOTES TO THE TEXT

(As a rule, a phonological or morphological peculiarity is explained on its first appearance only. Unless otherwise indicated, quotations from other works of Gil Vicente are taken from the *Copilaçam* and are transcribed in accordance with the same norms applied to the transcription of the *Floresta*).

Before line 1 (rubric). The word *foresta/floresta* entered the Hispanic world through the Peninsular versions of the French romances of chivalry, without, however, ever becoming popular since it did not correspond to any notion of a grove familiar to the Spanish and Portuguese people. As a poetic term, *foresta* "sucumbiu cedo à solicitação de *flor*, vindo *floresta* a ser... uma espécie de síntese entre a sombria *forest/forêt* germânico-francesa, e o *locus amœnus* florido" — Joseph Piel, *Miscelânea de etimologia portuguesa e galega* (Coimbra: Acta Universitatis Conimbrigensis, 1953), p. 170.

Before line 1 (rubric). "É vulgar nos documentos antigos, ainda quando antes da data se diz *era* ou *ano*, repetir *anos* no fim" — Leite de Vasconcelos, *Textos arcaicos* (Lisbon: Teixeira, 1922), p. 148.

1. *asegún*, 'según.' Occurs elsewhere in Vicente (cf. *infra*, line 95, and *Templo de Apolo*, fo. 161 a); it can also be found in Encina and Francisco de Avendaño's *Florisea* (Pedro Henríquez Ureña, *El Español en Santo Domingo*, Buenos Aires, Biblioteca de Dialectología Hispanoamericana, 1940, p. 83). The forms *asegún* and *asigún* are still alive in certain dialects (Henríquez Ureña, op. cit., p. 179, and Aurelio M. Espinosa, *Estudios sobre el español de Nuevo Méjico*, trans. Amado Alonso and Ángel Rosenblat, Buenos Aires, Biblioteca de Dialectología Hispanoamericana, 1930, I, 240-41). Medieval and Renaissance Portuguese texts register the form *a segundo*; see I. S. Révah, "Édition critique de l'*Auto de Inês Pereira*," *BHTP*, 5 (1954), 262, n. 314.

3. *gran pena le es conversar*: for the impersonal use of *ser* with an indirect object, see Hayward Keniston, *The Syntax of Castilian Prose: The Sixteenth Century* (Chicago: Univ. of Chicago Press, 1937), 2.631, 35.427, 37.231.

5. *sin lo poder escusar*: placing the object pronoun before the infinitive was a rather widespread practice in Spanish in the first half of the 16th century (Keniston, *Syntax*, 9.62 ff.). Juan de Valdés considers it "más llano y más puro y aun más galano y más castellano" to say *ponerlos, traerlas* than *los poner, las traer* — *Diálogo de la lengua*, ed. José F. Montesinos (Madrid: Espasa-Calpe, 1964), p. 157.

6. *antigos*, 'antiguos.' For examples of the use of this old form in Spanish, see Joseph E. Gillet, *"Propalladia" and Other Works of Bartolomé de Torres Naharro*, III (Bryn Mawr: Univ. of Penn. Press, 1951), 171, n. 227.

13. *passión*, 'apuros.' For *passión* in the sense of 'suffering,' very frequent in Torres Naharro and his contemporaries, see Gillet, *"Propalladia,"* III, 36, n. 26, and IV (Philadelphia: Univ. of Penn. Press, 1961), 355-57, and cf. *infra*, line 1028.

16. *en depués*, 'después.' Vicente uses both *depués* and *después*; the former is based on analogy with Portuguese *depois*; see Paul Teyssier, *La langue de Gil Vicente* (Paris: Klincksieck, 1959), p. 391.

17. *oído havéis*: though the auxiliary normally precedes the past participle in compound tenses, the order is sometimes inverted (Keniston, 33.9 ff.). The present case can be justified by the exigencies of the rime.

19. *ansí*, 'así.' Juan de Valdés prefers *assí* to *ansí*: "stá mejor la *s* que la *n*, la qual creo se ha metido allí por inadvertencia" (p. 84). *Comigo*, 'conmigo:' both forms are used in the 16th century, though the latter is more common (Keniston, 6.16).

26. *¿haste d'ir?*, '¿te irás?' *Haber de* is here a temporal auxiliary equivalent to the future (in the 16th century, the future was still seen as a combination of the infinitive and *haber*); the presence of the preposition may be explained by the vacillation, characteristic of the 16th century, between the pure infinitive and the infinitive with *de*. See Keniston, 34.44 and 34.445.

29. *hasta la mañana* means simply *mañana* (tomorrow) here as well as in line 58; it is an imitation in Spanish of the Portuguese *à manhã* (Teyssier, p. 395).

30-31. An explicit indication that the play is a Court entertainment and also that we are watching a play, not a scene from life.

33. *estuviéredes*, 'estuviereis.' The second person plural verbal proparoxytones retained the -d- as late as the 17th century. See Ramón Menéndez Pidal, *Manual de gramática histórica española*, 11th ed. (Madrid: Espasa-Calpe, 1962), 107,1, and Federico Hanssen, *Gramática histórica de la lengua castellana* (Halle: Niemeyer, 1913), 198. For a detailed discussion of such verbal forms in Vicente's Portuguese, see Teyssier, pp. 182 ff.

34. *hablá*, 'hablad.' Imperatives without final -d are common in 16th-century Spanish; see Pidal, *Manual*, 107,2, and Gil Vicente, *Tragicomedia de Amadís de Gaula*, ed. T. P. Waldron (Manchester: Manchester Univ. Press, 1959), n. 545. Juan de Valdés prefers the forms with final -*d* for two reasons, "por henchir más el vocablo," and to avoid confusion between two words spelled alike, "*toma*, con el acento en la *o*, que es para quando hablo con un muy inferior, a quien digo *tú*, y *tomad* con el acento en la *a*, que es para quando hablo con un casi igual, a quien digo *vos*" (p. 73). Cf. lines 766: *perdonáme*, 1065: *prendé*, 1204: *catá*.

35. *os diré de no*, 'os diré que no'. The use of *de* for *que* in similar elliptical expressions is very rare in the 16th century (Keniston, 42.483).

38 ff. The partitive *de* is frequently found in Vicente. Its use is only sporadic in 16th-century Spanish but quite the contrary in Portuguese: see Teyssier, pp. 332-33. Spanish examples are given by Gillet, III, 529, n. 178, and Keniston, 20.8 ff.

42. *el mi tormento*: this old pleonastic construction —still alive in Portuguese, Italian and Catalan— becomes scarce in Spanish in the 15th century

and disappears in the 16th, though it survives in legal documents, quotations from the Bible and in certain dialects. See Hanssen, *Gramática,* 517, and Keniston, 19.33. For examples, see Gillet, III, 37, n. 48.

43. *esquierdo,* 'torcido.' See the *Gran diccionario de la lengua castellana (de Autoridades),* ed. Aniceto de Pagés, 5 vols. (Barcelona: Fomento Comercial del Libro, n.d.) —hereafter cited as *Autoridades—* s.v. *izquierdo.* Initial pretonic *e* replaces *i* far more often in Vicente than in the Spanish writers of the time, a fact which can be attributed to the influence of Portuguese (see Teyssier, pp. 330-31). This particular case shows the influence of Portuguese *esquerdo.*

44-45. "Si quieres matar a un cuerdo, átale al pie un necio" (Gonzalo Correas, *Vocabulario de refranes y frases proverbiales,* Madrid, 1924, p. 459).

45. *atalde,* 'atadle.' The metathesis, which characterizes the fusion of the enclitic pronoun *le* with second-person-plural imperatives, persisted down to the classical period (Pidal, *Manual,* 115,3). Juan de Valdés disapproves of it: "tengo por mejor que el verbo vaya por sí y el pronombre por sí" (p. 50).

52-56. Note the nonsensicality of the *parvo*'s song, and see Teyssier, pp. 503-04, for additional cases of *disparates* in the *autos.* As Teyssier notes (p. 503), "le principe de tous ces morceaux est au fond le même: on laisse courir la plume au hasard des associations d'idées, et il en résulte une sorte de 'langage en liberté' qui, si l'auteur est en verve, pourra charrier dans son flot une multitude de détails imprévus et burlesques." Eduardo Martínez Torner in his *Lírica hispánica: Relaciones entre lo popular y lo culto* (Madrid: Castalia, 1966), p. 234, registers, together with this song, the following two *danzas de bastones,* the first from Oviedo and the second from Ávila: "Levántate, panadera, / si te quieres levantar, / que los hijos de Patricio / te vienen a pedir pan. / Yo les daré la mitad: / De cuatro panes que tengo / la mitad por el dinero, / la mitad por caridad. / Baila dichosa / panadera hermosa. / Que tran, que tran, / que tran, larán, larán."

"Levántate, panadera, / si te quieres levantar; / somos gente del Campillo, / venimos buscando pan. / ¡Ay jarandín, con el ay jarandán!"

52, 53. *Allevantes, llevantar* are not *sayagués* forms but *lusismos:* "le parallélisme *levar-levantar* du portugais est transposé en espagnol: comme cette langue dit normalement *levar,* on a créé la forme *llevantar.* C'est dans cette façon de maintenir le parallélisme des deux verbes que réside ici le lusisme." *Llevantar* occurs regularly not only in Vicente's Spanish texts but in those of other Portuguese writers (Teyssier, pp. 69, 74, 395). The prothesis of *a-* in the formation of verbs is a common phenomenon in both Old and Modern Spanish (Henríquez Ureña, *El español en Santo Domingo,* p. 199). Juan de Valdés remarks: "pongo *a* quando el vocablo que precede acaba en consonante, y no la pongo quando acaba en vocal, y assí, escriviendo este refrán, pongo: *Haz lo que tu amo te manda, y siéntate con él a la mesa, y no y asiéntate...* Pero, si no precede vocal, veréis que siempre pongo la *a,* como... aquí: *Allégate a los buenos y serás uno dellos*" (p. 54). For old and modern examples of *alevantar, alevantarse, allevantar,* see Henríquez Ureña, op. cit., p. 82, and Aurelio Espinosa, *Estudios...,* II (1946), 239-40. Contrary to Old Spanish usage, 16th-century Spanish writers do not use the second person of the subjunctive, with no introductory word, as a direct affirmative command —see Rafael Lapesa, *Historia de la lengua española,* 5th ed. (Madrid: Escelicer, 1959), p. 153, and Keniston, 29.171. Note, however, that this usage was very common in the *romances—* Rafael Lapesa, "La lengua de la poesía épica en los cantares de gesta y en el romancero viejo," *AdL*, 4 (1964), 8. Vicente who was immersed in them—his work is a mine of *romances*, whole and in fragments—may well have been influenced by this usage. Cf. also line 771: *saquéisme*, 'sacadme.'

54. Cf. Menéndez Pidal, *Flor nueva de romances viejos*, 20th ed. (Madrid: Espasa-Calpe, 1965), p. 282: "Que un cristiano dejo muerto" (from the "Romance de una morilla de bel catar"). J. P. Wickersham Crawford has shown that one of the traits of the *bobo* is his tendency to quote snatches of *romances*—see his "The *Pastor* and the *Bobo* in the Spanish Religious Drama of the Sixteenth Century," *RR*, 2 (1911), 400.

56. According to Gillet, *apiahá* is probably an "equivocal composite" of the Guaraní words *pïa* or *pïaá* (i.e. corazón) and *apiá* ("porrilla, y caput membri sine cute, como el circuncidado"), which were introduced into the Peninsula around 1530, and disappeared by the end of the century. "Attached to an exotic tune easily adapted to octosyllabic *pareados*, [*apiahá*] was at first the significant reiterated word (like *por qué* in the *Perqués*) at the head of each couplet. Later it might have been used to designate the tune to which any similar composition might be sung, or perhaps any composition in *pareados*. Erotically suggestive at first, and sung at country fairs to the accompaniment of humble instruments, it acquired a mingled flavor of rusticity and ruffianism, and eventually was lost in the meaningless formulism of a children's game." See his "Apiahá," *RPh*, 5 (1952), 316-18.

57. *dizid*, 'decid.' This is one of the many examples of vocalic assimilation (*e-i* > *i-i*) found in Vicente's Spanish; see Teyssier, pp. 325-26. It is also possible that in this particular case, the pretonic *i* is the analogical product of Portuguese *dizer*. *Hoje*, 'hoy': it is difficult to decide whether this *lusismo* was simply necessitated by the rime or whether it reflects a general tendency of Vicente's Castilian (Teyssier, p. 321).

57-58. Cf. Correas, *Vocabulario*, p. 235: "¿Haste de ir hoy? —No, sino mañana. —Pues vete por mi casa y echarte he una albarda. Manera de responder o reprender a los flojos y reposados y tardos."

62. *sofrirá*, 'sufrirá.' Instances of pretonic *o* for *u* are as frequent in Vicente's Spanish as in his Portuguese, and much more frequent than in contemporary Spanish authors (Teyssier, pp. 330-32). Among the latter, such vacillation in the quality of unstressed vowels gradually disappeared in the course of the 16th century (see Lapesa, *Historia*, pp. 189, 243); Juan de Valdés favors forms such as *ruido*, *cubrir*, etc. instead of *roído*, *cobrir* (p. 66). Vicente's usage may therefore be a *lusismo* (see Teyssier, loc. cit.).

63. *enhadará*, 'enfadará.' The same form occurs in the speech of Encina's rustics. The correspondence of Spanish *hado* and Portuguese *fado* may have led Vicente to adopt this form (see Waldron, *Amadís*, n. 140); he never employs the spelling *enfadar* (Teyssier, p. 371). *Enhadará... los desvaríos*: anacoluthon (for other instances of the same construction in this play, see lines 6-10, 94-98, 109-10, etc.).

68. *necedá*, 'necedad.' The loss of final *-d* is very frequent in Vicente, without suggesting any rustic or dialectal quality; see Gil Vicente, *Obras dramáticas castellanas*, ed. Thomas R. Hart (Madrid: Espasa-Calpe, 1962), p. 3, n. 36. See also Pidal, *Manual*, 35,4, and cf. line 812 of this play: *claridá*.

70. The *Copilaçam* of 1562—henceforth cited as "1562"—reads *otro*; it must be an error of the compositor, since its antecedent is clearly *necedá*.

71. *soy venido*, 'he venido.' Examples of the old use of *ser* as auxiliary in the formation of the compound tenses of intransitive and reflexive verbs can still be encountered in the 16th century. See Lapesa, *Historia*, p. 256, Keniston, 33.82, and Andrés Bello and Rufino J. Cuervo, *Gramática de la lengua castellana* (Buenos Aires: Anaconda, 1941), 1119.

76. *nuestramo*, 'nuestro amo.' A rustic form of address "aprendido en el teatro de aire leonés" — see A. Zamora Vicente's Introduction to his edition of Gil Vicente's *Comedia del viudo* (Lisbon: Centro de Estudos Filológicos, 1962), p. 36, and also n. 548.

81. *dormiesses*, 'durmieses.' The lack of inflection of pretonic *o* reflects a general vacillation in the Spanish of Vicente's time (see Teyssier, pp. 326-27, and Gillet, III, 43, n. 15, and 398, n. 61).

85. The entire line was removed in the *Copilaçam* of 1586; see A. Braamcamp Freire, *Vida e obras de Gil Vicente*, 2nd ed. (Lisbon: Rev. Ocidente, 1944), p. 413. The *Copilaçam* of 1586 will hereafter be cited as "1586".

86-88. Medieval astrology considered the phase of the moon at one's birth a decisive factor in one's fortune; see Waldron, *Amadís*, n. 70, and Joseph Piel, *Miscelânea*, p. 198 (I have been unable to consult the oftencited study by A. Faria Gersão Ventura, *Estudos vicentinos. I: Astronomia, Astrologia*, Coimbra, 1937). Cf. the "Romance de Abenámar" in M. Pidal's *Flor nueva*, p. 271: "el día que tú naciste / grandes señales había! / Estaba la mar en calma, / la luna estaba crecida; / moro que en tal signo nace / no debe decir mentira;" the proverb "Cuando menguare la luna, no siembres cosa alguna" (*Autoridades*, s.v. *menguar*); and Vicente's *Amadís de Gaula*, fo. 137 d: "... sirvo a Oriana, / hermosura soberana, / en cuyo nombre m'aparto / en dos partes y no en una: / la del alma doy a ella, / la del cuerpo a la fortuna / y a la luna / porque la hizo tan bella."

99. *aborrís*, 'detestáis.' "Verbe... employé plusieurs fois par Gil Vicente avec cette acception dans des textes en espagnol littéraire normal" (Teyssier, p. 37).

100. *vais*, 'vayáis.' The present subjunctives *vamos*, *vais* are still alive in the *Quijote* (Bello, *Gramática*, 582 and note). Cf. Juan de Valdés, p. 123: "el que compuso a *Amadís de Gaula* huelga mucho de dezir *vaiais* por *vais*; a mí no me contenta." In Vicente, the forms *vamos* and *vais* are more numerous than *vayamos*, *vayáis* (Teyssier, p. 326), perhaps because of the analogy with Portuguese *vamos*. Note that the old subjunctive *vamos* survives today in commands (M. Pidal, *Manual*, 116,5).

103. *por vos irdes escapando*, 'para escaparos.' One of the most distinctive characteristics of "Portuguese Castilian" is the transposition into Spanish of the Portuguese conjugated infinitive. See Teyssier, pp. 375 ff.

Before line 104. Sleeping on stage is one of Vicente's favorite comic devices, if we judge by the frequency of its occurrence. Cf. *Auto pastoril castelhano*, fo. 4 b, *Mofina Mendes* fo. 24 r, *Fama* fo. 198 c, *Juiz da Beira*, fo. 225 c, etc. For a discussion of this device in early Spanish drama, see W. S. Hendrix, *Some Native Comic Types in the Early Spanish Drama*, Ohio State Univ. Contributions in Languages and Literatures, No. 1 (Columbus: Ohio State Univ. Press, 1925), pp. 73 ff.

111. *no te isientes*, 'no seas altivo.' Vicente has made use here of the Portuguese verb *isentar* apparently in order to satisfy the demands of the

rime; furthermore, he has treated it as if it were a Spanish radical-changing verb.

116. *Coleo Romano*: "Quem será êsse legislador, ao qual obedece o filósofo... embora tivesse sido deshumano para êle?" wonders Carolina Michaëlis de Vasconcelos — *Notas vicentinas* (Lisbon: Rev. Ocidente, 1949), p. 394. Aubrey Bell suggests that this may be "uma alusão disfarçada ao Colégio Romano, o Sagrado Colégio dos Cardiais, e às dificultades de negociações entre D. João III e Roma, as quais terminaram pelo estabelecimento da Inquisição em Portugal, naquele ano (1536)"— *Estudos vicentinos*, trans. António Álvaro Dória (Lisbon: Imprensa Nacional, 1940), p. 173.

126-27. For a similar argument in favor of the use of prose, cf. *Auto da Lusitânia*, fo. 241 b: "E pera claro cimento, / e a obra nam ser escura, / direi em prosa o argumento." Vicente is one of the very few Peninsular dramatists before Lope de Rueda to make use of prose in a prologue; see J. A. Meredith, *Introito and Loa in the Spanish Drama of the Sixteenth Century* (Philadelphia: Univ. of Penn. Press, 1928), p. 93.

128. *peró*, 'pero.' "1562" reads *peroo*. The stress on the *o* is justified by the word's etymology (from Latin PER HOC); cf. Old Portuguese *perol*, Italian *però* and Catalan *però*. See Waldron. *Amadís*, n. 291.

After line 132. *un pobre escudero engañó un mercader*: Juan de Valdés is against the omission of the preposition *a* before accusatives, "porque sin la *a* parece que stán todos dos nombres en un mesmo caso," as is the case in *el varón prudente ama la justicia* (p. 157). The *lusismo* lies not in the construction itself but in the frequency with which it occurs in Vicente (see Teyssier, pp. 386-87). Note also the loose syntax of the *argumento*, frequent in the rubrics of "1562".

After line 132. *beúda*, 'viuda.' The form *veuda* occurs in the Marqués de Santillana — see *Cancionero castellano del siglo XV*, *NBAE*, 19 (1912), 525; and Corominas, *Diccionario crítico-etimológico de la lengua castellana*, 4 vols. (Bern: Francke, 1954-1957), s.v. *viuda*. The lack of other examples of the word in Spanish suggests perhaps that *beúda* is formed by analogy with Old Portuguese *veúva*.

143-44. Cf. Pedro Chaves, *Rifoneiro português* (Porto: D. Barreira, 1945?), p. 337, No. 680: "Quem dinheiro tiver fará o que quiser." The irony of the merchant's words becomes obvious in lines 256-57, where he realizes that "quem fôr tirano / tem seu dinheiro perdido." His initial attitude is responsible for his ultimate deception.

148. *misteirais*, 'artífices, mecânicos.' Old spelling of *mésteirais*; see Morais Silva, *Grande dicionário da língua portuguesa*, ed. Augusto Moreno et al, 10th ed., 12 vols. (Lisbon: Confluência, 1949-1954), s.v. *mesteiral*.

149. *estávão*: the only verbal form spelled in *-ão* in the play.

157. *pera*, 'para.' According to Said Ali — *Grammática histórica da língua portugueza* (São Paulo: Comp. Melhoramentos de São Paulo, 1931?), I, 250 — "a forma *pera* usou-se em todo o periodo do port. ant. e ainda no port. mod. do seculo XVI e principios do seculo XVII." See also Teyssier, p. 348.

160. *mexeriqueira*: "mulher que faz mexericos; enredadeira, intriguista" (Morais).

161. *mi*: old form of the pronoun *mim* (Morais, s.v. *mi*).

170. *is*, 'ides.' Archaic form. At the beginning of the 16th century there was vacillation in the use of these two forms; Vicente uses the first with

much greater frequency. For a detailed discussion of the verbal forms in -d- in the *autos*, see Teyssier, pp. 187 ff.

172. *nam-no*, 'não o.' In 16th-century Portuguese, both literary and popular, *no* was the normal form of the object pronoun after a nasal — A. Júlio da Costa Pimpão, ed., *Serra da Estrela* (Coimbra: Atlântida, 1963), p. 129; it still is after verb forms ending in a nasal.

175 ff. Cf. Correas, *Vocabulario*, p. 130: "La costumbre hace ley."

178. "Desusada no falar culto de hoje é a expressão negativa *até não* para significar 'emquanto não'. Topam-se bastantes exemplos desta linguagem em escriptores quinhentistas e alguns nos Sermões de Vieira:" Said Ali, *Grammática*, I, 229.

180. *embora*: a variant of *em boa hora*; *boa hora*, pronounced with elision of the final vowel of *boa*, gave *bo'ora* (*em bo'ora*), the result of contraction of the two *o*'s of which is *embora* (Teyssier, p. 497). This expression as well as its opposite (*em má hora, má-hora, em hora má, eramá, ieramá, eiaramá, aramá*) "sont nées d'anciennes croyances astrologiques: à certaines heures la conjonction des astres entraîne le succès et le bonheur, à d'autres l'échec et le malheur" (ibid., pp. 495 ff. See also Révah, *Recherches sur les œuvres de Gil Vicente. I. Édition critique du premier "Auto das Barcas"*, Lisbon, 1951, nn. 5, 15, 16). In Vicente, *embora* maintains its original meaning (i.e. it is not to be confused with modern Portuguese *embora*). Cf. lines 551 (*muitembora*) and 722 (*muitieramá*).

190. *mui*: apocopated form of *muito*; "só se emprega, geralmente, antes de adjectivos e advérbios começados por consoantes, e especialmente quando o advérbio modifica adjectivos tetrassilábicos ou longos advérbios sobretudo terminados em *-mente*" (Morais, s.v. *mui*).

191. *assi*: archaic form of *assim* (Révah, *Recherches*, I, n. 41). Teyssier translates this line: "aussi vrai que je souhaite ma propre vie, cela est la vérité!" (pp. 489-90).

195. *tisoureiro* is a popular form for *tesoureiro* (see Révah, *Inês*, n. 813); in the Portuguese of Vicente's time, *mor* and *maior* existed side by side; both are to be found in the *autos* (Teyssier p. 396). Today *mor* is used exclusively in poetic language and in the formation of compound titles such as *capitão-mor, sargento-mor*, etc. (Morais s.h.v.).

198. *tença*: "Quantia que o rei dava para sustento de um seu súbdito, por serviços prestados, mais vulgarmente aos cavaleiros que o haviam servido" (Morais, s.h.v.).

205. *corenta*, 'quarenta.' Old and popular form. See E. B. Williams, *From Latin to Portuguese*, 2nd ed. (Philadelphia: Univ. of Penn. Press, 1962), 40.7, and Morais, s.v. *corenta*.

208. *à menhám*: an old form for *amanhã*; see Révah, *Inês*, n. 723. *Manhã* gave *menhã* through a dissimilatory process in the late 15th or early 16th century (Williams, *From Latin*. 40.2A). *Sam*, 'sou.' The form *sam* of the first person singular of the Present indicative of *ser* was gradually replaced, during the 16th century, by *sou*. In Vicente, however, the former is still more frequent (Révah, Introduction to *Inês*, p. 101).

219. *tolo sandeu*, 'completamente louco.' Juan de Valdés believes that *sandio* was coined in Portugal; he affirms that it was not used in his day in Spain and is not sure whether it was ever used (p. 121). Covarrubias recognizes it as a "vocablo español desusado," and adds: "Díxose sandio de la palabra *insanus*, perdiendo la *in* del principio" — *Tesoro de la lengua*

castellana, ed. Martín de Riquer (Barcelona: Horta, 1943), s.v. *sandío*. Morais derives *sandeu* from Spanish *sandeo*. Corominas is uncertain of its origin, but thinks that it probably came from the phrase SANCTE DEUS "que pronunciada al principio como exclamación de piedad ante el pobre mentecato, acabó por aplicarse a este mismo" (s.v. *sandio*). Cf. the *romance* "Montesinos y Rosaflorida:" "O tenedes mal de amores / o estáis loca sandía" — Agustín Durán, ed., *Romancero general, BAE*, 10 (1849), 259, No. 384.

225. *bos*, 'bons.' Archaic and popular form; see Révah, *Inês*, n. 173, and Morais, s.v. *bô*.

226. *Jesu*: archaic for *Jesus* — Almeida Lucas, ed., *O velho da horta* (Lisbon: Ocidente, 1943), n. 57. *Aque* (from *aqui*) was formerly used in the standardized call for help *aque-del-Rei*!; see Morais, s.v. *aque*. The article *el* (from Latin ILLE, directly or through Spanish) is still used with the noun *rei*; see Williams, *From Latin*, 137.5, and cf. Teyssier, pp. 156-57.

228. *rezões*, 'razões.' The *e* is the product of dissimilation which occurred in the late 15th or early 16th century (Williams, *From Latin*, 40.2A). It was perhaps influenced also by the great number of words which begin with the prefix *re-*.

229. *amara*, 'amarga.' *Amaro* (from Latin AMARU-): old form of *amargo*; see Morais, s.v. *amaro*.

233. *no-mais*, 'não mais.' The old form *nom* of the negative adverb, united proclitically to *mais* and without its nasalization, was preserved as late as the last part of the 16th century; see Epifânio da Silva Dias's edition of *Os Lusíadas*, III, 67 (cited by Morais, s.v. *no*). See also Révah, *Inês*, n. 576.

Before line 238. *despois*, "depois.' Archaic and popular form; see Almeida Lucas, *Velho*, n. 275, and Révah, *Recherches*, I, n. 837.

Before line 247. *veo* 'veio.' Archaic form. The diphthongized form emerged in the 16th century, though both continued to be used for a long while. Vicente uses them both indiscriminately. See Almeida Lucas, *Velho*, pp. 101-02, and Révah, *Inês*, n. 146.

266. This is a line of a 16th-century *villancico* registered by Menéndez Pidal in his *Romancero*, p. 52 (see Marques Braga's edition of Vicente's complete works, III, 180, n. 25). Cf. also "De Gil Vicente a el-Rei dom João terceiro" (fo. 261 d): "¿A quién contaré mis quexas, / gran Señor, / a quién contaré mis quexas / si a vos no?," and *Comédia de Rubena*, fo. 87 d: "¿A quién me descubriré, / a quién contaré mi pena?"

275. *tanto ha*, 'tanto tiempo hace.' Sixteenth-century Spanish regularly uses the verb *haber* in expressions indicating the period of duration of a state or action (see Keniston, 32.13 ff., and 36.911).

283. This line, especially when combined with line 300, is reminiscent of the fact that Christ's death on the Cross was caused by man's sinfulness. Cf. Isaiah, 53.5: "Ipse autem vulneratus est propter iniquitates nostras, attritus est propter scelera nostra; disciplina pacis nostrae super eum, et livore eius sanati sumus;" and Peter, I, 2.24: "Qui peccata nostra ipse pertulit in corpore suo super lignum; ut peccatis mortui, iustitiae vivamus: cuius livore sanati estis." Interspersed in Cupid's speech — in particular — are distant echoes of the Bible, which would be blasphemous if they were more direct. In "1586" this line reads: "Pues que a tu rey tienes muerto." See Braamcamp Freire, p. 413

284. *arrepiéndete*, 'arrepiéntete.' Vicente has probably confused Spanish *arrepentirse* with Portuguese *arrepender-se*.

291. *pecador*, 'pecadora.' By Vicente's time, the feminine forms in *-ora* had been standardized in Spanish, whereas Portuguese still retained the forms in *-or*; hence *pecador* may be an archaism or a *lusismo*. Vicente uses the forms in *-or* but only in rime (Teyssier, pp. 335-36).

293. This line was modified in "1586" to: "que mataste al Rey damor;" see Braamcamp Freire, p. 413.

301-02. Teyssier translates these lines: "ce sera pour toi une pénitence suffisante que de penser à mon tourment" (p. 377). For the use of the conjugated infinitive in Vicente see note to line 103.

303. *merecimento*, 'merecimiento.' *Lusismo*; Vicente elsewhere uses the diphthongized form (Teyssier, p. 364).

311. The omission of the definite article before *dios* may be justified by the exigencies of the meter.

316. *norabuena*, 'en hora buena.' There are numerous cases of apheresis in Vicente; they are the result of the influence of Portuguese. The form *norabuena* is used much more often than *en hora buena* (Teyssier, pp. 367-69). Cf. also *namorado, naquella* (lines 318, 450).

318. *eres namorado*, 'estás enamorado.' In 16th-century Spanish, the difference in the use of *ser* and *estar* to indicate the resultant state of an action was not yet firmly established (Lapesa, *Historia*, pp. 256-57).

330. *terná*, 'tendrá.' Some of the old syncopated future forms survived until the 16th century; among these are *tenré* (through metathesis *terné*), *porné* (cf. line 689), *verné* (cf. line 786). See Pidal, *Manual*, 123,2, and Hanssen, *Gramática*, 261.

331. *risco*, 'riesgo.' This *lusismo* does not appear elsewhere in the Spanish portion of Vicente's work; it may be used here solely for the sake of the rime (see Teyssier, p. 322).

332 ff. Cupid's words remind one of the prophets' warnings, in the Old Testament, of the ultimate destruction of Israel owing to her people's lapses into sin. Cf., for example, Isaiah, 1.7: "Terra vestra deserta, civitates vestrae succensae igni: regionem vestram coram vobis alieni devorant, et desolabitur sicut in vastitate hostili." Cf. also the *Auto da Cananea*, fo. 83 a, and the "Carta a el-Rei dom Joam o terceiro," fo. 257 v, in which Vicente refers to the destruction of Sodom and Gomorrah, and of Jerusalem by Nebuchadnezzar. The affliction and imminent desolation of the city of Thebes, and the conditions for its saving in *Oedipus Rex* offer another parallel to the present situation. Vicente might have acquired knowledge —direct or indirect— either of Sophocles' story of Oedipus or, more likely, of Seneca's version: in addition to the 15th-century manuscript editions and translations in Spanish and Catalan of the latter's tragedies — see Menéndez y Pelayo, *Bibliografía hispano-latina clásica*, ed. Enrique Sánchez Reyes, vol. VIII (Santander: Aldus, 1952), 42, 51, 52, 62— there was Brocar's printed edition of *Senecae tragoediae*, Alcalá, 1517; see F. J. Norton, *Printing in Spain: 1501-1520* (Cambridge: Cambridge Univ. Press, 1966), pp. 42 and 203.

333. *a barrisco*, 'completamente.' "Mot de la langue familière générale appartenant aux deux langues hispaniques [portugais et espagnol], et employé dans le sayagais comme un élément de style populaire" (Teyssier, p. 37). Covarrubias derives it from *barrer*: "Barrer todo lo que ay es

llevárselo sin cuenta ni razón, y desta semejança se dixo también llevarlo todo a barrisco." See also Corominas, s.v. *barrer,* and Gillet, III, 216, n. 196.

335. *tiene hecho tantos males*: though the past participle, in compound tenses formed with *tener,* normally agrees with the direct object, there are certain 16th-century constructions in which it remains invariable; see Keniston, 33.881.

341. Cf. Correas, p. 567: "El remedio está en la mano."

345-348. The idea of the mountain as a site of penitence is a familiar one: it reminds one of the mountains of Judea on which Jephthah's daughter was sent to prepare for two months for her sacrifice (Judges, 11.30-11.40), of Christ's frequent withdrawals to the mountains for prayer and meditation, and, of course, of Dante's Purgatory.

346. *serra Minea,* 'sierra Minea.' A fictitious mountain (Carolina Michaëlis, *Notas,* p. 456). In the *Comédia de Rubena* (fo. 92 b), "Minea" is the name of one of the *fadas. Serra* is obviously a *lusismo.*

354. *ablasado,* 'abrasado.' Under the influence of Portuguese, *r* after a consonant is occasionally confused with *l* in Vicente's Spanish (see Teyssier, pp. 359-60).

355-359. Cf. Matthew, 10.39: "Qui invenit animam suam, perdet illam: et qui perdiderit animam suam propter me, inveniet eam;" also 16.25, Mark, 8.35, Luke, 9.24, 17.33, and John, 12.25.

358. *oferecida,* 'ofrecida.' *Lusismo.* Both *ofrecer* and *oferecer* are found in Vicente's Spanish (Teyssier, p. 351).

362. *haze,* 'haz.' *Lusismo;* the correct form of the imperative (*haz*) also occurs in Vicente (Teyssier, p. 384).

365-369. These lines appear in five of the six extant copies of "1562". "Los esfuerzos que se han tenido que hacer... para embutir estos cinco versos en el folio después de iniciada la tirada, los garantizan como auténticos" — Stephen Reckert, "El verdadero texto de la *Copilaçam* vicentina de 1562," StPh, 3 (1963), 60.

370. *adó,* 'adonde.' One of the variants of the relative adverb *donde,* still surviving in poetic and popular language (see Hanssen, *Gramática,* 661, 669, and Bello, *Gramática,* 394 ff.). Other variants in this play: *onde* (*adonde,* line 443) *ónde* (*dónde,* 689); one should not classify them as *lusismos,* for they were used in the Spanish of Vicente's time (see Teyssier, p. 327).

371. *estó,* 'estoy.' To satisfy the demands of the rime, Vicente makes occasional use of the old first-person-singular forms *estó* (estoy), *vo* (voy), *so* (soy); see Teyssier, p. 326, and cf. Juan de Valdés: "*Yo so, por yo soy,* dizen algunos, pero, aunque se pueda dezir en metro, no se dize bien en prosa" (p. 121).

372. *entrementes,* 'entretanto." This *lusismo* does not occur anywhere else in Vicente (Teyssier, p. 363). According to Corominas (s.v. *mientras*), this form may simply be a cross between *entretanto* and (*de*)*mientre,* "a no ser que se quiera partir de una reduplicación INTERIM-INTERIM del latín vulgar."

375. *erro,* 'yerro.' *Lusismo* for lack of diphthongization (Teyssier, p. 363).

Before line 385. "ao deos" was omitted in "1586" (Braamcamp Freire, p. 413).

385. Cf. Erasmo, *El Enquiridion* — though the resemblance may seem fortuitous in the light of Marcel Bataillon's conviction that "si Gil Vicente pudo leer a Erasmo, ciertamente no sacó de él nada para su teatro:" see

his *Erasmo y España*, trans. Antonio Alatorre (Mexico: Fondo de Cultura Económica, 1950), II, 213 — p. 128: "Tú, por ventura, quando oras solamente tienes ojo a quantos salmos mal rezados has passado por la boca, y piensas que en el mucho parlar está puesta *toda* la virtud de la oración. Y este es un vicio principalmente de aquellos que aún son como niños principiantes en la letra sin levantarse ni crecer a la madureza del espíritu. Mas oye lo que en este caso nos enseña Christo por Sant Matheo: Quando oráredes no curéys de multiplicar muchas palabras, como hazen las gentes que no conocen a Dios, que piensan ser oydos por su mucho hablar. No queráys vosotros parecer a éstos, pues sabe vuestro padre celestial lo que avéys menester antes que se lo pidáys. Y Sant Pablo tiene en más cinco palabras bien sentidas y que salgan del coraçón que diez mill pronunciadas assí solamente por la lengua" — ed. Dámaso Alonso and Marcel Bataillon (Madrid: Centro de Estudios Históricos, 1932). Juan de Valdés makes an analogous case: "el ardiente desseo del ánima hiere las orejas de Dios, que no el estruendo ni la muchedumbre de las palabras" — see his *Diálogo de doctrina christiana*, ed. Domingo Ricart (Mexico: Univ. Nacional de México, 1964), pp. 90 f. Cf. also the *Refranero clásico español*, ed. Felipe Maldonado (Madrid: Taurus, 1960), p. 44, No. 147: "La oración breve sube al cielo." For a comprehensive study of Vicente's conception of prayer as it manifests itself in his work, see António José Saraiva, *História da cultura em Portugal*, II (Lisbon: Jornal do Fôro, 1953), 333-39.

386. *sancto*, 'santo.' It was the practice of the writers and especially the printers of the Renaissance to adopt the Latin and Greek spelling of words, with "utter disregard for pronunciation." Such a tendency had begun even before the 16th century (Williams, *From Latin*, 31). Cf. also lines 391, 437, and 513.

392-393. Cf. Correas, pp. 369: "Obras son amores, que no buenas razones," and 46: "El amor y la fe, en las obras se ve." For a comprehensive exposition of the supremacy of *action* over *word*, with Medieval and Renaissance examples, see Gillet, IV, 90-104 and 296-97.

398-399. Line 398 is omitted in five of the six extant copies of "1562"; "se podría pensar quizá en una modificación editorial (acaso de Luis Vicente) motivada por la serie de tres versos monorrimos" (Reckert, "El verdadero texto," pp. 60-61). As a result, line 399 is modified, in the same copies, to: *que no puede menos ser* (ibid., p. 61).

405. *longo*, 'luengo.' A *lusismo*; the correct spelling *luengo* is also found in Vicente's Spanish (Teyssier, p. 365).

411. "Verecinta está por Berecinta, nacionalização de *Berecynthia*; adjectivo gentílico (como Cytherea) apôsto à *alma mater*, ou Rhea ou Kybele ou Ops, isto é, à *Terra* fecunda e mãe dos deuses; e é tirado do monte Berekynte na Frígia, que era sagrado à grande deusa, mùlher de Saturno" (Carolina Michaëlis, *Notas*, p. 345). While almost all of Vicente's gods derive from Juan de Mena's *Coronación*, his knowledge of Verecinta comes from Fray Antonio de Guevara's *Marco Aurelio*, twice printed in Portugal before 1530; see Eugenio Asensio, "El *Auto dos Quatro Tempos*," *RFE*, 33 (1949), 372 and note. *Julia* is probably an error for *Juno* (C. Michaëlis, *Notas*, p. 323; see also p. 421). "Da helénica Pallas-Athene, e da sua correspondente latina, sabia o comediógrafo tão pouco que faz figurar ambas como divindades diversas na invocação da *Lusitânia*; Minerva como advogada da fermosura, e Pallas, sem outra caracterização do que *diesa*" (ibid., p. 437).

419. *de nos,* 'de nosotros.' In the middle of the 15th century, the personal pronoun *nosotros* became prevalent over the simple form *nos,* which, however, survived down into the 16th, particularly in the first decades. Torres Naharro offers numerous examples of *nos* both as subject and as prepositional object; additional examples are furnished by Juan del Encina and others. See Gillet, III, 61-62, n. 63, and Keniston, 4.11 and 4.12.

420. *diesas,* 'diosas.' A hypercorrect form based on the gallicism *dees(s)a,* which was frequent in Old Spanish and Portuguese — see Thomas R. Hart, *Obras castellanas,* p. 82, n. 327, and María Rosa Lida de Malkiel, *Juan de Mena, poeta del prerrenacimiento español* (Mexico: NRFH, 1950), p. 248. The dissimilation of the *e* of *deesa* may be due to the influence of *dios.*

445. *dell ánima,* 'del ánima.' Vicente's Castilian texts offer sporadic examples of the article with palatalized *l* before masculine or feminine nouns beginning with a vowel (see Waldron, *Amadís,* n. 338). This primitive usage occurs also in Torres Naharro — particularly in the speech of his rustics — Villalobos, Cisneros, and Alfonso de Valdés (see Gillet, III, 245, n. 113, and Keniston, 18.126 ff.).

452. *mucho en breve serán*: there are occasional examples in the 16th century of *mucho* modifying adjectives, adverbs or adjectival and adverbial phrases, instead of *muy* (Keniston, 39.6). Vicente employs this construction less often than that with *muy,* but still more often than contemporary Spanish authors; in Portuguese, both constructions, with *mui* and *muito,* were equally alive (Teyssier, pp. 329-30). Cf. line 544: "lugar mucho secreto."

454. In early Spanish ballads, pastoral poetry, and drama, *amarillo* is used as a symbol of "sadness, despair, loss of hope, or trouble of any kind." See H. A. Kenyon, "Color Symbolism in Early Spanish Ballads," *RR,* 6 (1915), 332 *et passim.* And cf. Correas, p. 42: "Amarillo color, desesperación. Porque el trigo y mieses verdes dan esperanza de cogerse, y por eso lo verde significa esperanza; mas cuando ya están granadas y amarillas, no hay más que esperar; de aquí nació tomar la color amarilla por desesperación, como parece que se seguía, no hay que esperar, mudando lo que era ser lograda en desesperada, y desconfiada de ser alcanzada." Cf. also *Cortes de Júpiter,* fo. 167 d: "Irá outra linda estrêla / sobre carreta d'estrêlas, / vestida toda amarela / porque desesperem dela, / como das outras donzelas."

455. The adverbial construction *muy mucho* — used as an emphatic form of *mucho* — is current in the 16th century. See Keniston, 39.74.

461. *vuesso,* 'vuestro.' According to Keniston (19.16), this form is found in the 16th century only in the expression *vuessa merced.* Cf. Juan de Valdés, pp. 91-92. Leif Sletsjöe has studied the distribution of *vuesso* and *nuesso* in the Spanish portion of Vicente's dramatic work; he concludes that the alternation of *vuesso* and *vuestro* is of considerable significance in establishing the chronology of the *autos* of the first period — see his "Los posesivos *nuesso* y *vuesso* en el español de Gil Vicente," *RJ,* 16 (1965), 274-89.

464. *se estilan,* 'se destilan.' *Estilar* occurs frequently in medieval and Renaissance Spanish (as early as the 'Fuero de Arguedas,' 1092, and as late as after Fray Luis de León); it survives in Andalusia, Salamanca and South America. See Gillet, III, 104, n. 19.

476. *como se,* 'como si.' *Se* instead of *si* can be found in old Leonese texts, and 16th-century Spanish writers employed it in the speech of their rustics (Gillet, III, 671, n. 380); the frequency of its use in Vicente and

the other Portuguese writing in Spanish, however, suggests that it is a *lusismo* (see Teyssier, p. 335).

486. *cobdicia,* 'codicia.' Cf. *Libro de buen amor,* 218a: "De todos los pecados es rrayz la cobdiçia." Consonantal groups such as *-bd-* can still be found in writings of the first half of the 16th century, though the first consonant was no longer pronounced (Lapesa, *Historia,* p. 244). Juan de Valdés shows preference for forms like *cobdo, cobdiciar, dubda, súbdito* (p. 69).

490. *lo tengo de mío,* 'como mío.' The strong possessive adjectives are used idiomatically in partitive constructions with *de.* Cf. Alonso Enríquez de Guzmán, *Libro de la vida y costumbres,* 143,15: "estos maravedís he buscado prestados, por do creereis que cuando los tenga de mios, os dare más" (quoted in Keniston, 19.992). See also Hanssen, 700.

Before line 497. Carolina Michaëlis cannot make sense of these Latin words which, though correct in themselves, are completely disconnected (*Notas,* pp. 231, 290). Such a disparity, however, should not be taken as a reflection of Vicente's knowledge of Latin. Costa Ramalho has shown in two articles — "Uma bucólica grega em Gil Vicente," and "Algumas observações sobre o latim de Gil Vicente," both in *Humanitas,* 15-16 (1963-1964), 328-47 and 17-18 (1965-1966), 198-210 — that the playwright, contrary to Carolina Michaëlis' contention, was able to read both classical and ecclesiastical Latin; Eugenio Asensio had already expressed, though not as positively, a similar opinion in his "Las fuentes de las *Barcas* de Gil Vicente," *BHTP,* 4 (1953), 212. Concerning Vicente's treatment of Latin, Costa Ramalho believes (see the first of the two cited studies, p. 329) that "pôr latim incorrecto na boca de personagens cultivados e, inversamente, latinidade correcta na fala dos incultos era uma prática que decerto divertia o próprio Gil Vicente e não só ele. Entre os espectadores, muitos se ririam da partida pregada à gravidade dos latinistas encartados do tempo."

497. *buscaes,* 'buscáis.' The forms in *-aes* are the first result of the loss of intervocalic *-d-* which occurred in the 15th century (with respect to the second-person-plural verbal paroxytones); see Pidal, *Manual,* 107,1, and Hanssen, 198.

500. *jagora,* 'agora mesmo.' The product of elision of *já* and *agora.* Cf. Morais, s.v. *já*: "se todos partem, *já agora,* também parto."

509. *dereito,* 'direito.' Archaism (Révah, *Recherches,* I, n. 611; see also Almeida Lucas, *Velho,* n. 409).

515-516. Certain scholars have seen autobiographical evidence in these lines, assuming, quite arbitrarily, that the dramatist appeared in the role of the Chief Justice (Aubrey Bell, however, believes that it might have been Garcia de Rèsende, who "aos outros talentos acrescentava o de actor" and who died at Évora in 1536 at the age of sixty-six—*Estudos vicentinos,* p. 77, note). Since the play was composed in 1536, they locate Vicente's birth in 1470. But others claim, with equal arbitrariness, that Vicente most likely had the leading part in the *Velho da horta* (1512); three lines, addressed to the *velho* ("Havei, má-hora, vergonha / a cabo de sesenta anos, / que sondes já carantonha," fo. 204 a), move the playwright's birth date to 1452 (!). For a more extensive discussion of these unfounded hypotheses, see Braamcamp Freire, pp. 48-49. See also Óscar de Pratt — *Gil Vicente: notas e comentários* (Lisbon: Teixeira, 1931), pp. 69-70 — who, taking as point of departure a passage from the *Auto da Festa,* arrives at 1465 as the approximate year of Vicente's birth; this is the most widely accepted date.

517. *havés,* 'haveis.' *-és* for *-eis* was common in the first part of the 16th century; it suggests no dialectal quality in Vicente, for it occurs in the speech of characters of all categories. See Teyssier, pp. 173-74, and Óscar de Pratt, *Gil Vicente,* pp. 63-64.

523. This line was replaced in "1586" by: "porque me matais com isso" (Braamcamp Freire, p. 413). Cf. *O Velho da horta,* fo. 202 b: "Vindes vós, meu paraíso...".

525. *improviso,* 'improvisamente.' The adjective is used here in an adverbial sense. Cf. Gaspar Correia, *Lendas da India,* I, 609: "logo mandou um seu criado polos rios dentro com sua carta... contando o que os Mouros fizeram tão acidentalmente, e tão *improviso,* que se não pudera socorrer" (cited in Morais, s.v. *improviso*).

528. Cf. *O Velho da horta,* fo. 203 a: "minhas flores...".

533. *fermosa,* 'formosa.' The usual form in the 16th century; see Révah, *Recherches,* I, n. 380, and Almeida Lucas, *Velho,* n. 111.

539. *e qué...,* 'y qué....' Though many old Spanish texts regularly employ the form *e* for the copulative conjunction (see Hanssen, 679), this is most likely a *lusismo de imprenta.*

543. *privar,* 'tener privanza, aislarme.' Berceo uses *privanza* in the sense of "diálogo, conversación íntima;" see Rufino Lanchetas, *Gramática y vocabulario de las obras de Gonzalo de Berceo* (Madrid: Sucesores de Rivadeneira, 1900).

556. *antre,* 'entre.' Archaic form (Révah, *Recherches,* I, n. 153).

557. *assoviaes,* 'assobiais.' Classical form of *assobiar* (Révah, *Inês,* n. 785; see also Morais, s.v. *assoviar*).

558. *tamalaves,* 'um pouco.' "Encontrável uma ou outra vez em algum autor quinhentista ou seiscentista, o advérbio *tamalavez* entra no rol dos vocábulos de emprego raro. Não se pode afirmar que é reliquia de uso anterior mais generalisado, porque faltam as provas" (Said Ali, *Grammática,* I, 221; among the examples cited is this line). See also Carolina Michaëlis, "Miscelas etimológicas," *HMPi,* III, 466 ff.

562. *jantar,* 'yantar.' Portuguese authors who wrote in Spanish often confuse the Spanish equivalents of Portuguese *j*; see Teyssier, p. 372.

566. *formento,* 'fermento.'

568. *negro,* 'maldito.' Covarrubias tells us (s.h.v.) that *negro* "es color infausta y triste, y como tal usamos desta palabra diziendo: Negra ventura, negra vida, etc." According to Teyssier (p. 439), *negro* occurs very frequently in the *autos.* Particularly surprising is the recurrence of the term in this scene (see lines 567, 633, 664, 666, 667, 694). Combined with the circumstances within which the main portion of this episode unfolds, namely the time, and the Justice's impersonating a negro baker-woman, such an apparently conscious repetition helps to envelop the figure of the Justice with an aura of infamy, and to foreshadow his disgrace.

570-571. Fragment of a *cantiga* popular in 16th-century Portugal (see Marques Braga, *Obras completas,* IV, 248, nn. 16-18). According to Beau, this song foretells what is going to happen — "A música na obra de Gil Vicente," in his *Estudos* (Coimbra: Acta Universitatis Conimbrigensis, 1959), I, 230. Cf. *Cortes de Júpiter,* fo. 168 a: "Enganado andais, amigo, / comigo, / dias há que vo-lo digo."

575. *mao,* 'difícil.' This spelling is the result of the hiatus which occurred through the loss in Portuguese of intervocalic *-l-*. See Williams, *From Latin,* 48.2A, and Erma Learned, *Old Portuguese Vocalic Finals*

(Baltimore: Linguistic Society of America, 1950), 4b, 13, 40, 42. *Mao* appears again in line 640.

584. *condón*, 'poder mágico.' It is the Castilianized form of Portuguese *condão* of which there is no exact Spanish equivalent. "Quand existe en portugais un moyen d'expression sans équivalent exact en castillan, Gil Vicente ne cherche pas à 'traduire', c'est-à-dire à exprimer la même idée avec d'autres mots: il se contente de castillaniser le terme portugais:" Teyssier, pp. 390-91. The same is also true of line 956. Cf. *Rubena*, fo. 88 a: "¡Quién tuviera, o quién hallara / una preciosa vara / que tuviera tal condón...!"

586. *rienda*, 'rinda.' Diphthongized forms of the verb *rendir* occur in Torres Naharro, among others. See Gillet, III, 100, n. 97, and Teyssier, p. 328. And cf. line 622: *riendo*, 'rindo.'

598. *item mais*, 'outrossim.' A term of medieval notarial language, *item* was particularly used to introduce a new paragraph in testaments or contracts — Leo Spitzer, "Salmantino en *íteles* y *véntiles*," RFH, 8 (1946), 130. Cf. *O pranto de Maria Parda*, fo. 261 b: "Item mais, mais mando dar...."

601. *beatilha*: "touca de pastoras e de beatas ou freiras, donde a tal lençaria tomou o nome" (Morais, s.h.v.).

610-612. Cf. *Refranero clásico español*, p. 34, No. 116: "Todas las cosas quieren maña," and Correas: "Todo ha menester maña, sino el comer que quiere gana;" "Todo este mundo es trazas y trapazas" (p. 481); "A todo hay maña, sino a la muerte" (p. 69). Cf. also *infra*, lines 924-25.

624. *dulcis amor qui me vis?*, '¿qué me quieres, dulce amor?' The correct form of the Latin interrogative pronoun is *quid*. Carolina Michaëlis (*Notas*, p. 259) has apparently confused the episode of the usurious merchant with this one, and has consequently mistaken these words as being addressed "à mocinha de uma viúva fingida."

626. *este lavor*, 'esta labor.' In Portuguese *lavor* is masculine, whereas in Spanish it has remained feminine; in the *autos*, it is always treated as masculine. See Teyssier, p. 384.

629. *asinha*, 'de pressa.' From Latin AGĪNA, *asinha* "figura tanto em verso como em prosa, culta e popular, desde os primeiros monumentos da literatura... até quasi fins do seculo XVII." Today, it can be found in dialects. See Carolina Michaëlis, "Miscelas," p. 469.

632. *perro* was the most common insult used when referring to a Negro as well as to a Moor or a Jew — Frida Weber de Kurlat, "Sobre el negro como tipo cómico en el teatro español del siglo XVI," RPh, 17 (1963), 390.

633. *geito*, 'gesto.' From Latin *iactus*, geito originally meant "act of throwing," hence "skill, ability;" but it also took on the connotations of "manner," "attitude," "demeanor," "appearance." With this spelling it is found in old texts, particularly in Fernão Lopes. *Geitas*, 'lanças, arremessas' (from *iactāre*), in line 637, is an archaic verb. See Yakov Malkiel, "Latin *iactāre*, *dēiectāre*, and *ēiectāre* in Ibero-Romance," BdF, 10 (1949), 209-10; and cf. *Inês Pereira*, fo. 219 d: "pera nos geitar por riba."

640. Cf. Covarrubias s.v. *aojar*: "Qüestión es entre los phísicos si ay mal de ojo, pero comúnmente está recebido aver personas que hazen mal con sólo poner los ojos en otra, especialmente si es con ira o con embidia; y desta mala calidad de empecer con la vista fueron infamadas algunas naciones. En África huvo una gente que destruía las cosas, con sólo mirarlas, secando los árboles y matando los animales... Oy día se sospecha que en España ay en algunos lugares linages de gentes que están infamados

de hazer mal poniendo los ojos en alguna cosa y alabándola, y los niños corren más peligro que los hombres por ser ternecitos y tener la sangre tan delgada, y por este miedo les ponen algunos amuletos o defensivos y algunos dixes, ora sea creyendo tienen alguna virtud para evitar este daño, ora para divertir al que mira. Ordinariamente les ponen mano de tasugo, ramillos de coral, cuentas de ámbar, pieças de cristal y azabache, castaña marina, nuez de plata con açogue, rayz de peonia y otras cosas.... Todo esto es superstición y burla... Verdad es que no de todo se reprueva la opinión de que ay mal de ojo." The belief in the malign influence of the evil eye (*mau olhado*) is still very much alive in Portugal; for details about it and for a description of the great variety of amulets used against it, see Rodney Gallop, *Portugal: A Book of Folk-Ways* (Cambridge: Cambridge Univ. Press, 1961), pp. 59, 60, 61, 63, *et passim*. The aspect of witchcraft in connection with the evil eye is treated by Vicente in *Rubena* (fos. 88-89 — included is an exorcism against the *quebranto*). Meteo 'meteu.' By the beginning of the 16th century, the *-o* of the ending of the third singular preterit — which had been much earlier established in "a sporadic and haphazard way" — had been generally replaced in writing by *-u*. See Williams, "Old Portuguese *-eo*," *BdF*, 11 (1950), 61, and Erma Learned, *Old Portuguese Vocalic Finals*, and cf. *vio* in line 672.

641-647. Though the Negro jargon used by the Judge does not contain so many phonological, morphological, and syntactical peculiarities as do other similar passages in Vicente — understandably, since this is only an imitation of Negro speech — it is still distorted enough to merit special attention. According to Teyssier, the passage is in "petit nègre espagnol," "un espagnol... d'ailleurs bourré de lusismes qui, s'ajoutant à la syntaxe enfantine et à la morphologie rudimentaire, accentuent l'impression exotique" (p. 243). Verbs are invariably in the infinitive: *estar, bradar, llamá* (with the latter's final *-r* dropped); *a* and *o* in final unstressed position are confused: *destemplado, tudo, hablanda* (though the false rime in 645-646 suggests that the latter may be a misprint); there is confusion in the quality of pretonic *e* and *u* in *Furnando*. The stressed possessive adjective *mía* precedes the noun *señora*, which may be a *lusismo*; the prepositional construction *a mí* has taken the place of *yo me* (in line 646). Finally, there is a great number of lexical *lusismos*: *tudo* (toda), *peneirada* (cernida), *bradar* (rallar), *cousa* (cosa), *cadela* (perra), *nam* (no). For an extended discussion of the traits of Negro speech in literature, both before and after Vicente, see Teyssier, pp. 227-50. Whenever the negro speaker is referred to by name, whether in Vicente or in some later dramatists, the name is invariably *Fur(u)nando* (Fernando); Vicente, therefore, may be credited with the creation of a comic type (see Teyssier, pp. 249-50).

642. *tanto*, 'tan.' *Tanto* before a past participle is rare in the 16th century (Keniston, 39.87).

649. *patorneando*, 'parolando.' Archaic verb. See Morais, s.v. *patornear*, and cf. *Auto da feira*, fo. 34 c: "iremos patorneando."

651. *bolorento*: "velho, antigo, decrépito, decadente, acabado" (Morais, s.h.v.).

654. *milhor*, 'melhor.' Old literary form. The palatalization of *l*, produced by the *yod*, caused the *e* to close to *i*. See Williams, *From Latin*, 41.3A, and Costa Pimpão, *Estrela*, p. 127. This old spelling better represents the pronunciation of the word then as now. Cf. also line 719.

663. *co*: contraction of the preposition *com* and the article *o*. It survives only in certain dialects; see Almeida Lucas, *Velho*, n. 284, and Williams, *From Latin*, 137.4B.

664. In order to avoid the obvious obscurity in the sense of the line, it is necessary to emend the reading *negras* of "1962" to *negro*, as the editors of Vicente's complete works have invariably done.

667. "1562" reads *ouidores* which is evidently a misprint — it is possible that the compositor confused and contracted the two consecutive *u*'s, without realizing that the first was a vowel and the second a consonant. *Ouvidor* was the "juiz togado que ouvia e sentenciava com outros as causas e pleitos que ocorriam nas audiências" (Morais, s.h.v.). It is interesting to note that here the Chief Justice has become, in essence, the defendant, as a result of his having exceeded the boundaries of his jurisdiction.

674. *dizede*, 'dizei.' Archaic form of the second person plural of the imperative. The forms in *-ade, -ede, -ide* were popular in Vicente's time (Révah, *Recherches*, I, n. 750).

676. *Bártolo*: "o grande professor e jurisconsulto de Bolonha (1313-1357) que compôs o primeiro *Comentário do Direito Romano*;" Carolina Michaëlis, *Notas*, p. 381. Cf. Correas, pp. 297 ("Más sabe que Bártulo"), 370 ("Oficio tiene Bartolo para el día todo"); Correas also registers the expression "arrimar los bártulos," meaning "dejar el estudio; bártulos son los libros" (p. 536).

679. *micelos*, 'desgraciados.' All the editors of Vicente's complete works have read *Y mis celos*, considering it an elliptical phrase. Aubrey Bell, on the other hand, has timidly suggested (*Estudos vicentinos*, p. 173) that *micelos* may be from Latin *mĭsellus*, diminutive of *mĭser*. His derivation, though phonologically irregular (-S->-c-, -ELLU>-elo), resolves the problem of meaning whereas the other editors' interpretation cannot be sustained by the context, as there is no reason to assume any jealousy on the part of the Judge. In addition, the omission of the *-s* in *mi celos* is also phonologically irregular. Another factor which leads us to adopt Bell's view is the reappearance of the term, with the same meaning, in the *Romagem de Agravados*, fo. 187 b: "E por parecer miselo / e toda a côrte em mi crea, / defumo-me co este zelo, / e faço o rosto amarelo / com muita palha centea."

689. *penera*, 'cedazo.' An attempt to transpose into Spanish the Portuguese *peneira*, by eliminating the diphthong *ei*. See Teyssier, p. 397.

692. Note that the pretonic *a* of *pàdeira* is open in Modern Portuguese: see Entwistle, *The Spanish Language: Together with Portuguese, Catalan and Basque* (London: Faber and Faber, 1936), pp. 300-01, and Williams, *From Latin*, 40.9, 60.1, 99.2B.

693. *Baldo*: Baldo de Ubaldis, "célebre jurisconsulto italiano (1324-1406), discípulo de BÁRTOLO. Tornou-se costume citá-los juntos. Na Alemanha dizemos mesmo em casos difíceis que 'nem Baldo nem Bártolo nos pode valer';" C. Michaëlis, *Notas*, p. 380. Cf. the "Dezir que fizo Juan de Mena sobre la justiçia:" "Ally es Bartolo e chino digesto, / Juan Andres e Baldo" — in *Cancionero castellano del siglo XV*, *NBAE*, 19 (1912), 200.

696-698. The mention of the powerful Chaldean king — Bucodonosor through apheresis — as an authority in support of the *velha's* words, is definitely burlesque (in the *Auto da Lusitânia*, fo. 243 b, mention is made of the "psalteiro de Nabucdonosor"). What is important here, however, is the play on the words *cans* and *canas*: *can* is equivalent to Spanish *cana*; but there is also a Portuguese *cana* corresponding to Spanish *caña*. "Grâce à la paire luso-castillane *cã-cana* les 'cheveux blancs' du vieux juge deviennent des 'roseaux', des 'roseaux creux', — façon de dire que, malgré son âge, il est bien étourdi et léger. L'expression prend toute sa saveur grâce à l'adjectif *vão*, qui en portugais signifie 'vide, creux', en même temps que 'vain, futile'..., et grâce aussi à l'existence de l'expression *cana vã*, qui désigne une espèce de roseau;" Teyssier, p. 412; see also Carolina Michaëlis, *Notas*, p. 434.

700. *má*, 'mau.' Archaic and popular form (see Morais, s.v. *mau*).

703. *per quam regula*, 'com que direito.' As is the case with most Latin phrases in the text, this is incorrect: it should be *regulam*. See Carolina Michaëlis, *Notas*, pp. 235, 288 (Dona Carolina has erroneously attributed these words to the "escudeiro disfarçado em velha" — p. 288). Cf. *Auto das fadas*, fo. 208 d: "*Per quam regula* diremos?" *Micer*, 'meu senhor.' The origin of the term can be sought, through Catalan *misser*, in dialectal Italian *misser*. In 15th and 16th-century Spanish it referred to Italians and Catalans (see Corominas, s.v. *señor*). *Micer* is also registered in Portuguese (see Morais). Coming from the *velha*'s lips, it is full of mock courtesy; it appears with similar force in the *Auto da Índia*, fo. 196 d: "Falai vós passo, micer."

705. *nas piós*, 'nas correias.' "Incham os pés algumas vezes aos falcões por terem as *piós* apertadas, e de mau couro:" Diogo Fernandes Ferreira, *Arte da Caça*, II, 4, Ch. 19, 30 (cited in Morais, s.v. *pió*). Cf. *Lusitânia*, fo. 240 d: "num aito bem acordado / que tenha ave e piós."

706. *mana minha!*, 'que graça!, que jocoso!' An exclamation in which the word *mana* — from Latin GERMANAM, reduced by its proclitic position — has lost its etymological meaning (Almeida Lucas, *Velho*, n. 183); see also Gillet, III, 253-54, n. 29.

710. *uma pouca*, 'um pouco [de farinha].' Keniston registers several examples in 16th-century Spanish in which the pronoun *un poco de* agrees with the noun which depends upon *de*, and has the force of an adjective (13.1). Additional Spanish examples are furnished by Gillet (III, 448-49, n. 107), who notes that the construction occurs also in Portuguese.

719. *veo*, 'véu.' See note to line 575.

720. *en*, 'em.' Archaic form; see Morais, s.v. *en*.

726. *veludo*, 'velludo.' This may be a *lusismo de imprenta*; it is the only example of the word in Vicente (Teyssier, p. 369).

730. *ervilhastes*, 'endoidecestes.' See Morais, s.v. *ervilhar*: "ter desejos disparatados e inoportunos."

733. The pretonic *e* of *prègar* is open in Modern Portuguese (see Williams, *From Latin*, 41.13, 60.2). *Altemira*: "em Portugal não há, que eu saiba, lugares dêsse nome. Há *Altemiras* diversas em Espanha. Ignoro todavia qual delas deu origem à locução: *ir prègar a Altemira*, no sentido de bater a outra porta" (Carolina Michaëlis, *Notas*, p. 374). Note the omission of the preposition *a*, which however may be merely orthographic, since an initial *a-* follows.

740. According to Carolina Michaëlis, *Sena* stands for *Siena* "depois de Bologna, a mais afamada das Universidades italianas onde se estudava direito" (*Notas*, p. 455). We tend to agree, however, with Aubrey Bell who interprets it as a synecdochical reference to Paris — see his *Studies in Portuguese Literature* (Oxford: Oxford Univ. Press, 1914), p. 62. The

Chief Justice has already referred to the University of Paris (cf. *supra*, line 625).

744. *y irme*, 'e irme.' The use of the conjunction *e* before *i*- was not yet firmly established. As Gillet notes (III, 11, n. to p. 137, line 15), Torres Naharro was beginning to use *e* for *y* before *i*- though not before *hi*-.

753. There are a few examples, in the early 16th century, of compound tenses formed with *haber*, in which the past participle is in agreement with the direct object; see Keniston, 33.87.

757. *Apolo Dios*: when a noun was in apposition with another noun in 16th-century Spanish, it frequently became adjectival and did not need the definite article (Keniston, 18.2). The word *Dios* was replaced by *a nos* in "1586" (Braamcamp Freire, p. 413).

760. *sacreficio*, 'sacrificio.' The product of a dissimilatory process characteristic of Portuguese and of Old Spanish. Both forms occur in the *autos* (Teyssier, p. 325).

768. *en medio desta defesa*: cf. also lines 809-10 ("en esta brava floresta / y entre estas espessuras"), 898-99 ("yo me voy por aquí / a oír los ruisinoles"), 992-93 ("se me perdem as vacas / sem pastor"), 1088 ("esta floresta"), 1092 ("este desierto"), 1094 ("por sierra tan sin concierto"), 1112 ("por tan áspera montina"). By means of such references, Vicente creates "the desired impression of an outdoor mountain scene" —R. B. Williams, *The Staging of Plays in the Spanish Peninsula Prior to 1555*, Univ. of Iowa Studies in Spanish Language and Literature, No. 5 (Iowa City: Univ. of Iowa, 1935), p. 47. Although some of Vicente's plays make use of pageant devices, in general there is a striking absence of décor. The temporal and spatial ambience within which the action unfolded was established mainly by means of the dialogue, movement and costumes; the audience's imagination was, of course, required. See Óscar de Pratt, *Gil Vicente*, pp. 41-48, and also N. D. Shergold, *A History of the Spanish Stage from Medieval Times Until the End of the Seventeenth Century* (Oxford: Clarendon Press, 1967), pp. 40-41, 133-36, and 167-68, *Defesa*, 'dehesa.' This form occurs in medieval Spanish writings, including the *Libro de buen amor* (298a: "Un cavallo muy gordo pascía en la defesa"); in the 14th and 15th centuries, however, *dehesa* became frequent. See Corominas, s.v. *dehesa*. The present case is probably a *lusismo*.

772. *fuistes*, 'fuisteis.' *-es* was the normal ending of the second person plural of the preterit in 16th-century Spanish; see Pidal, *Manual*, 107,3 and 120,5, and Teyssier, p. 326.

777. *saludad*: the adaptation in Spanish of Portuguese *saudade*. Gil Vicente uses several different forms of the word, both in Spanish and in Portuguese (*soledad, saludad, suidade*). See Teyssier, pp. 400-02, and cf. *O Triunfo do Inverno*, fo. 181 cd: "de saludades minero," "em suidades me mantens," "suidade me faz sentir," "A suidade na molher / mata o coraçám e alma."

778. *ansí como ansí*, 'de una manera y otra.' "Es muy usada frase" (Correas, p. 533). For examples of the use of this expression, see the *Autoridades*, s.v. "así como así."

783. *mandar*, 'mandare.' The future subjunctive was regularly used in 16th-century Spanish. Here, and on several occasions in his Spanish texts, Vicente employs its forms without *-e*, as in Portuguese; see Teyssier, pp. 373-74.

789. *vicio*, 'placer, holganza.' This was the usual meaning of the term in Old Spanish; for examples see Gillet, III, 623, n. 66. Cf. also Correas, p. 68: "A sus once vicios: por muy a su placer."

791. *pera*, 'para.' It must be a *lusismo*.

798. *acabas*, 'consigues, logras.' See A. Zamora Vicente, *Viudo*, n. 731.

804. *prefeción*, 'perfección.' The metathesis of *r* in prefixes such as *per-* and *por-* is very common in Portuguese and in Vicente's Spanish (see Teyssier, pp. 351-56). As to the preservation or simplification of the Latin consonantal group -CT- "ni siquiera a fines del siglo XVII existía criterio fijo:" Lapesa, *Historia*, p. 249. Cf. line 1054.

811. In "1586", *el cielo* was substituted by *mi casa* (Braamcamp Freire, p. 413). *A escuras*, 'a oscuras.' The most frequently encountered form in Medieval Spanish and up to the Golden Age (see Corominas, s.v. *oscuro*).

819. *tengo de*, 'tengo que.' *Tener de*, as an auxiliary expressing necessity, was much more common in the 16th century than *tener que*. See Keniston, 34.82 and 34.83.

824. *fierros*, 'hierros.' Vicente's Castilian often preserves initial etymological *f-* for stylistic reasons in words which begin with *h-* in Modern Spanish; here, however, there seems to be no special stylistic flavor (Teyssier, pp. 370-71).

831-833. These lines were omitted in "1586" (Braamcamp Freire, p. 414).

837-838. Porqueras Mayo notes that the origin of the *topos* "no haber nacido" (the first Spanish example of which dates back to the first part of the 13th century—in *Vida de Santa María Egipciaca*—and which is very frequently found in 15th-century poetry before reaching its artistic fullness in Calderón) is Biblical: "Pereat dies in qua natus sum" (Job, 3.3); see his "Nuevas aportaciones al topos 'no haber nacido' en la literatura española," *Segismundo*, 3 (1967), 63-64. The same formula occurs frequently in Gil Vicente, too; cf. *Auto da India*, fo. 195 d: "pese al día en que nascí;" *Rubena*, fo. 88 d: "¡Oh, quien no fuera nascida!;" *Velho da horta*, fo. 203 c: "Oh, quem nam fôra nacido!," and also *supra*, lines 86-88.

838. *nasci*, 'nací.' Though the etymological group *sc* is found in archaic forms of the verb (see the *Autoridades*, s.v. *nascer*), this must be a case of analogy with Portuguese *nascer*.

847. *dezillas*, 'decirlas.' Throughout the 16th century, the assimilation of the final -*r* of the infinitive to the initial *l-* of the following third-person object pronoun was a common phenomenon (Keniston, 9.611). Juan de Valdés concedes that "lo uno y lo otro se puede dezir," though he prefers the unassimilated forms (pp. 82-83).

853. The word *dios* is omitted in "1586" (Braamcamp Freire, p. 414).

876. *nadia*, 'nadie.' This cross between *nadie* and *nada* was often used by all the Portuguese who wrote in Spanish; see Teyssier, p. 396.

880. In "1586", this line reads: "del palacio no uiniera" (Braamcamp Freire, p. 414).

883. There are examples, in 16th-century Spanish, of the subjunctive in a principal clause in expressions of entreaty (Keniston, 29.111). This type of construction, in which the object pronoun precedes the verb of entreaty, tends to disappear in the second half of the 16th century. The position of the object pronoun is justified here by the fact that the verb follows a stressed element, the subject (ibid., 9.541).

888. The meter seems to be responsible for the missing definite article before *lágrimas*.

893. *cred,* 'creed.' A very frequent *lusismo* in Vicente and the other Portuguese authors who wrote in Spanish; it is the result of the reduction of etymological *ee* in the Portuguese verbs (Teyssier, p. 380). Cf. also lines 1087, 1143.

899. *ruisinoles,* 'ruiseñores.' A variant form of *ruiseñor,* which is a corrupt derivative of Vulgar Latin LŪSCĪNĬŎLUS, diminutive of Classical Latin LUSCINIA or LUSCINIUS: "en romance, la primera L se cambió por disimilación, y en castellano el vocablo se alteró por una etimología popular, que lo interpretó como si fuese *Ruy señor* 'señor Rodrigo'" (Corominas, s.v. *ruiseñor*).

901 ff. Cf. the *parteira*'s words in *Rubena,* fo. 89 a: "Há hi homens tam sobejos / que, má trama que lhes naça, / com enganos, com despejos, / lá buscam má-hora ensejos / pera êles tomarem caça."

902-905. Cf. Alfonso Martínez de Toledo, *Corbacho,* ed. Lesley Byrd Simpson (Berkeley: Univ. of Calif. Press, 1939), p. 198: "¡Maldita sea la que jamas en onbre se fia, amen!," and Tirso's *El burlador,* ed. Américo Castro (Madrid: Espasa-Calpe, 1922), iii, 394: "¡Mal haya la mujer que en hombres fía!" Tirso repeats the same phrase in *La Santa Juana* — see *Comedias de Tirso de Molina,* ed. Emilio Cotarelo y Mori, *NBAE,* 9 (1907), 294.

910. *se remerita,* 'se merece.' *Remeritar* is probably an intensive form of *meritar,* which, according to Corominas (s.v. *merecer*), "parece galicismo entrado por Cataluña, donde se empleó algo en el S. xvi; hoy lo emplean algunos en el sentido neológico de 'mencionar, hacer mérito.'"

916. *huelo,* 'sospecho.' For this figurative meaning of *oler,* see the *Autoridades* ("conocer ó adivinar una cosa que se juzgaba oculta"). "1562" reads *buelo,* obviously a misprint.

920. "1562" has *do* which must be a misprint.

922. *reñiego,* 'reniego.' This is not a *sayagués* form, though it appears to be: the palatalization of the *n* is the result of assimilation to the following *yod*; see Teyssier, p. 69.

929-930. That love is an overpowering force which the individual cannot resist, is a recurrent idea in Vicente. Cf. *Rubena,* fo. 98 d: "que a Dios plaze / que amemos en tal lugar," *D. Duardos,* fo. 136 d: "amor me lleva / que no fue la culpa mía," and also *supra,* 620-622. It is course ironic here for the god of love himself to suggest such a thing.

931-939. Cupid's invective against women, combined with lines 1052-1056, is in the tradition of the debate — so popular in 15th- and 16th-century Spain — regarding the relative imperfections and virtues of women. The arguments against them and in their favor were ultimately drawn, according to Arturo Farinelli, from Boccaccio's *Il Corbaccio* and *De claris mulieribus* respectively; see Wickersham Crawford, *The Spanish Pastoral Drama* (Philadelphia: Univ. of Penn. Press, 1915), p. 86. Cf. also the lengthy debate, on the same issue, between Fileno and Cardonio in Encina's *Égloga de tres pastores,* in *Églogas,* ed. H. López Morales (New York: Las Américas, 1963), lines 297 ff., the first of its kind in the Spanish drama (Crawford, loc. cit.).

934. *destruición,* 'destrucción.' This form was used as late as *Don Quijote*; see Corominas, s.v. *construir.*

941. The reference here is to St. Saturninus. The Catholic Church recognizes four saints by this name. It is most likely that Vicente was thinking of the French martyr who was the first bishop of Toulouse in the 3rd century, and who was condemned by the pagan priests to die dragged by

a bull through the streets of the town. He is the only one of all four whose name is legendarily associated with the beginnings of the church of San Sernín at Pamplona — see the *Enciclopedia de la religión católica*, 7 vols. (Barcelona: Dalmau y Jover, 1950-1956), s.v. *Saturnino*. The shepherd has distorted the spelling of the saint's name which in Portuguese in *Sadorninho*. Cf. *Quem tem farelos?*, fo. 194 a: "Oh mártere Sam Sadorninho!," and *Rubena*, fo. 89 c: "Dou-vos a Sam Sadorninho."

948. *Castelhano* is here used in a derogatory sense; see Teyssier, p. 294 and note, and cf. *Serra da Estrêla*, fo. 174 a: "Agora nos faria o demo / a nós outros castelhanos? / Queria antes ser lagarto, / pelos sanctos avangelhos!"

950. *qués*, 'quieres.' *Lusismo* for *quiés*, "sans valeur stylistique spéciale" (Teyssier, p. 117 and note). *Quiés* occurs in Torres Naharro and even in prose: see Gillet, III, 790, n. 196.

970. Cf. the expression "valer una cosa un Perú" meaning "ser de mucho precio ó estimación" (*Autoridades*, s.v. *Perú*).

973. *buena prol te haga*, 'que te aproveche.' *Prol* is the Portuguese equivalent of Spanish *pro* (see Teyssier, p. 399). Cf. Covarrubias, s.v. *pro*: "palabra antigua que vale provecho, y assí dize el pregonero, quando remata en almoneda alguna cosa: Que buena pro le haga."

986. *bofá*: contraction of *à boa fé*. "Fórmula de juramento com que se asselava a veracidade do alegado, correspondendo por tanto a *em verdade, decerto*" (Costa Pimpão, *Estrela*, p. 117). *Bofá*, a popular form, derived euphemistically from *bofé*: "la langue cherche à masquer ce qu'une expression de ce genre peut avoir de sacrilège en la rendant méconnaisable" (Teyssier, p. 141). *Enxoval*, 'espertalhão.' See Costa Pimpão's glossary of his edition of the *Obras completas* (Barcelos: Editora do Minho, 1956).

990. "1562" has *binir*, possibly due to an accidental inversion of *u*. *Bivir* is required by the sense of the line. Moreover, the forms of *venir* are spelled in this play with *v*, whereas it is the compositor's practice to dissimilate two *v*'s within the same word, writing the first as *b*: *bivir, bolver*, and so on.

991. *cadea*, 'cadeia.' "Até o século XVI, era essa a pronúncia e a grafia usada, não se verificando a ditongação em *ei*, por não corresponder à pronúncia do tempo." Vicente uses both spellings (Almeida Lucas, *Velho*, pp. 101-03; see also Révah, *Inés*, n. 368).

997. *pesar de*: "forma impessoal que introduz diversas locuções interjectivas, de dor ou desgôsto;" Almeida Lucas, *Velho*, n. 268. See also Révah, *Recherches*, I, n. 235.

1002. *desfaçamo-lo*, 'desfaçamos o.' The final *s* of the second singular and first and second plural verb forms was regularly assimilated, in Old Portuguese, to the following *l* of the primitive form of the article *lo* (from Latin ILLUM); the long *l* remained short. Modern Portuguese has not retained this combination except dialectally; see Williams, *From Latin*, 137.3, and J. Dunn, *A Grammar of the Portuguese Language*, Hispanic Society of America Publications, No. 230 (Washington, D. C.: National Capital Press, 1928), 62b. Modern Portuguese has retained, however, the same combination with the object pronoun; e.g. *ama-lo* (amas-o): see Dunn, 229c-f, 386.

1004. *vene*, 'viene.' *Lusismo* for lack of diphthongization (Teyssier, p. 363). It is the only undiphthongized form of this verb in the play.

1005. *pardeos!*, 'por Deus!' "Juramento, de largo emprego literário e popular, desde a fase arcaica da língua" (Costa Pimpão, *Estrela*, p. 130); see also Keniston, 43.34, and Gillet, III, 345, n. 143.

1006. *corpo de mim*: a very common type of interjection in Vicente's time. See Almeida Lucas, *Velho*, n. 294, Révah, *Inês*, n. 532, Keniston, 43.34, and cf. the numerous examples of the same and similar expressions listed in Gillet, III, 344-45, n. 130. In the present case, *corpo de mim* expresses anger.

1009. *indino*, 'indigno.' Archaic and popular form (Morais, s.v. *indino*).

1022. *esprementar*, 'experimentar.' Although the syncope of pretonic vowels in contact with *r* had become rare in Spanish by the early 16th century, Vicente generally allows himself the same freedom of treatment in Spanish as in Portuguese. In many places in the *autos*, such pretonic vowels are retained but only in spelling (i.e., they do not affect the meter); see Teyssier, pp. 345-51, and, for analogous Spanish examples, Gillet, III, 120, n. 132, and cf. the *Auto das fadas*, fo. 207 b ("quanto tenho esprementado") and 212 a ("por esprementar ventura").

1036. *pessoa*, 'ninguém.' Medieval and Renaissance Spanish texts offer a number of examples in which *persona* is used with negative force, like French *personne* (see Gillet, III, 691, n. 326, Keniston, 40.65, and E. L. Lloréns, *La negación en español antiguo*, Madrid: Centro de Estudios Históricos, 1929, par. 86). It is likely, then, that this is a case of *castellanismo*. Cf. *O Triunfo do Inverno*, fo. 175 a: "sem pessoa preguntar;" note also that the statement "nam sou ninguém" is the key to salvation for the *parvo* of the *Barca do inferno* (fo. 45 d).

1037. *soltar-mè*, 'soltai-me.' There are many instances of the infinitive with imperative force in Vicente; see Révah, *Recherches*, I, n. 465, and Almeida Lucas, *Velho*, n. 330.

1053. *a una mano*, 'de conformidad.' See the *Autoridades*, s.v. *mano*, and cf. Correas, p. 538: "todos a una mano salían buenos o malos. Esto es, conformes, como si por una mano fueran hechos o escogidos."

1061. *ni es razón*, 'ni hay razón.' Keniston lists 16th-century examples, in which *ser* is used with the force of impersonal *hay* (35.61).

1062. *estea*, 'esté.' This is the only case in Vicente where *estea* instead of *esté* is found. "En portugais le subjonctif présent de *estar*, qui était *esté*, forme parallèle au castillan *esté* a été remplacé par *esteja* par analogie avec *seja*. A l'époque de Gil Vicente *estê* et *esteja* sont employés côte à côte... Notre *estea* castillan n'est autre qu'une forme analogique faite sur *sea* comme en portugais *esteja* est fait sur *seja*" (Teyssier, pp. 383-84).

1070. This line is missing in "1586" (Braamcamp Freire, p. 414). *Lo ál*, 'lo demás.' Covarrubias informs us that "en la lengua castellana antigua, vale ál lo que cerca de los latinos *aliud*, y es muy ordinario en los mandatos de los señores dezir: E non fagades ende ál, so pena de la nuestra merced; y un cantarcillo dize: *Tango vos, el mi pandero, / Tango vos, y pienso en ál.*" Juan de Valdés cites the proverbs *So el sayal ay ál*, and *En ál va el engaño* but he states that personally he uses *otra cosa* instead of *ál* (p. 105). After 1530, *ál* is only sporadically used; see Keniston, 13.1.

1071. *vé*, 'ved.' Though "1562" has *ve*, all the editors of Vicente's complete works have read *veis*. For the frequency of imperatives without final *-d*, see *supra*, n. 34.

1074. *algún hora*, 'alguna hora.' The apocopated form of the qualifying adjective may be here due to analogy with the expression *en buen hora* — for which see note to line 1128.

1086. If we remember that the sibyl Casandra, in the homonymous *auto* (fo. 12 d), has used exactly the same words to address the Virgin, Cupid's utterance may sound blasphemous. It was, however, a common practice of the poetry of the time, to utilize in the language of love terms and conceits pertaining to the realm of religion. See Teyssier, pp. 450, 472. For medieval and Renaissance examples of the deification of women, see Gillet, IV, 337 ff.

1094. *concierto*: a term from hunting; see the *Autoridades*, s.v. *concertar*: "visitar el monte y los lugares fragosos de él, y por la huella y pista, saber la caza que en él hay, el lugar donde está y la parte donde ha de ser corrida."

1098. *pelegrino*, 'peregrino.' An archaic form; see the *Autoridades*, s.v. *pelegrino*.

1102. Cf. Torres Naharro, *Aquilana*, IV, 693: "un hijo del rey de Vngría." Gillet tells us that in the "early sixteenth century Hungary was a distinctly 'romantic', far-off country, all the more sympathetic to Spaniards as it was fighting, on land, the struggle against Islâm, which for Spain, on the sea, was to culminate at Lepanto" (III, 805, n. 693).

1105. *genelosía*, 'genealogía.' The same variant form occurs in the Marqués de Santillana's *Bías contra Fortuna* (Gillet, III, 651-52, n. 58).

1112. *montina*, 'montaña.' *Montiña* is an archaic form of *montaña* (see the *Autoridades*, s.v. *montiña*). The depalatalized form *montina* may be the result of "analogical confusion:" Portuguese *nh* often corresponds to Spanish *n* (e.g. *galinha* : *gallina*, *vinho* : *vino*). Such correspondence may have led the author or the printer to believe that *montina* was the correct Spanish form. The same form appears again in the *Triunfo do Inverno*, fo. 175 d: "tómales la noche / naquella montina."

1114-1115. Among the various roles ascribed to Fortuna in the Middle Ages was that of a guide. There are numerous references, in which "she is responsible in one way or another for *bringing* man into some particular place or set of circumstances" — see H. R. Patch, *Goddess Fortuna in Mediaeval Literature* (Cambridge, Mass.: Harvard Univ. Press, 1927), Ch. iii, esp. p. 99.

1120. *vido*, 'vio.' An archaic form still alive in popular and dialectal speech (see Pidal, *Manual*, 120,5, and Henríquez Ureña, *El español...*, pp. 52, 90, 176). Cf. Correas, p. 423: "Quien me vido algún tiempo y me ve agora, ¿cuál es el corazón que no llora?," and p. 427; also *La Celestina*, ed. Julio Cejador y Frauca (Madrid: Espasa-Calpe, 1963), II, 43: "¡Ay, quien me vido e quien me vee agora, no sé cómo no quiebra su coraçón de dolor!"

1122. *lémbreos*, 'acordaos de.' *Lembrar* is one of the popular variants of *membrar* (from Latin MĚMŎRARE) and reflects the influence of Portuguese *lembrar*, also a derivative of *membrar* through the dissimilated Leonese *nembrar*. The forms *lembrar* and *alembrar* occur in Sebastián Fernández's *Policiana* and Torres Naharro's *Calamita* respectively (see Corominas, s.v. *membrar*, and Gillet, III, 689, n. 219).

1128. *en buen hora*, 'en buena hora.' This apocopated form of *bueno* occurs, in the 16th century, not only before masculine nouns, but also, occasionally, before feminine beginning with *a*-, and in the expression *en buen hora* (Keniston, 25.225).

1152. *holgara*, 'holgaría.' For examples of the use of the imperfect subjunctive in -*ra* with potential force in 16th-century Spanish, see Keniston, 29.94 and 32.85 ff.

1155. *el alegría*: it was a common practice in the 16th century to use the definite article *el* before feminine nouns beginning with unstressed *a* (Keniston, 18.123).

1165. The definite article was evidently omitted before *dios* to avoid a hypermetric line.

1178 ff. Cf. *Serra da Estrêla*, fo. 172 d: "O casar Deos o provê / e de Deos vem a ventura, / da ventura à criatura...;" and Correas, p. 109: "Casamiento y mando, del cielo es dado."

1183. Cf. *Libro de buen amor*, 697c: "Dios é la mi ventura;" Correas, p. 525: "A Dios y a ventura, 'cuando nos arrojamos a lo dudoso en confianza que Dios ayudará, y podrá haber buena suerte;'" p. 637: "Quiso Dios y norabuena." Also, *Comédia do viúvo*, fo. 106 b: "Dios y la ventura quiso;" *Quem tem farelos?*, 194 a: "quis Deos e minha ventura;" "Ao Conde do Vimioso," fo. 258 a: "quis Deos ou a fortuna."

1192. "A fama do reino antigo [de Pérsia] perdura nas novelas de cavalaria e de lá passou às comédias" (Carolina Michaëlis, *Notas*, p. 440).

1194. *pracera*, 'parcera, compañera.' This form is found in medieval as well as in Golden Age writings; under the influence of the expression *ir a partir* or of the verb *apartir* ('tener parte, participar'), this form was replaced in Spanish by *aparcero*; see Corominas, s.v. *aparcero*.

1195. *aplaze*, 'gusta, agrada.' Archaic form for *placer* (from Latin PLACĒRE); during the Middle Ages, *placer* was the exclusive vehicle of this idea; its synonyms *agradar* and *gustar* were introduced later, in the 15th and 16th centuries respectively (Corominas, s.v. *placer*).

1207-1208. Cf. Correas, p. 273: "Lo que puedes hacer hoy, no lo dejes para mañana, no;" and p. 272: "Lo que has de hacer cras, pon la mano y haz. Que no lo dejes para mañana."

1211-1212. A proverb; see Virginia Joiner, "Proverbs in the Works of Gil Vicente," *PMLA*, 57 (1942), 69-70, where she cites an analogous example from Rodríguez Marín's *Más de 21.000 refranes castellanos* (Madrid, 1926), p. 150: "El casamiento del tío Porra, que duró treinta años y no llegó la hora."

After line 1212 (colophon). "1586" does not include the following words: "... dêste Segundo Livro, e a derradeira..." (Braamcamp Freire, p. 414).

BIBLIOGRAPHY

Abbreviated publications:

AION-SR:	*Annali dell' Instituto Universitario Orientale di Napoli (Sezione Romanza).*
AdL:	*Anuario de Letras.*
BAE:	*Biblioteca de Autores Españoles.*
BCom:	*Bulletin of the Comediantes.*
BdF:	*Boletim de Filologia.*
BHS:	*Bulletin of Hispanic Studies.*
CN:	*Bulletin d' Histoire du Théâtre Portugais.*
BRAE:	*Boletín de la Real Academia Española.*
CN:	*Cultura Neolatina.*
DHR:	*Duquesne Hispanic Review.*
HMPi:	*Homenaje ofrecido a Menéndez Pidal.* 3 vols. Madrid: Librería Hernando, 1925.
HR:	*Hispanic Review.*
MLN:	*Modern Language Notes.*
MP:	*Modern Philology.*
NBAE:	*Nueva Biblioteca de Autores Españoles.*
NRFH:	*Nueva Revista de Filología Hispánica.*
PMLA:	*Publications of the Modern Language Association of America.*
PQ:	*Philological Quarterly.*
RFE:	*Revista de Filología Española.*
RFH:	*Revista de Filología Hispánica.*
RJ:	*Romanistisches Jahrbuch.*
RomN:	*Romance Notes.*
RPh:	*Romance Philology.*
RR:	*Romanic Review.*
SP:	*Studies in Philology.*
StPh:	*Studia Philologica: Homenaje ofrecido a Dámaso Alonso por sus amigos y discípulos.* 3 vols. Madrid: Gredos, 1960-1963.
TDR:	*Tulane Drama Review.*

ALONSO, DÁMASO and JOSÉ M. BLECUA. *Antología de la poesía española: Poesía de tipo tradicional.* Madrid: Gredos, 1956.

ALONSO, DÁMASO. "El hidalgo Camilote y el hidalgo Don Quijote." In his *Del Siglo de Oro a este siglo de siglas.* Madrid: Gredos, 1962, pp. 20-28.

Alonso, Dámaso. "La poesía dramática en la *Tragicomedia de Don Duardos*." In his *Ensayos sobre poesía española*. Madrid: Rev. de Occidente, 1944, pp. 125-44.

———. "Un lusismo de Gil Vicente." *RFE*, 24 (1937), 208-13.

Andrews, J. Richard. "The Harmonizing Perspective of Gil Vicente." *BCom*, 11 (Fall 1959), 1-5.

Artola, G. T. and W. A. Eichengreen. "A Judeo-Portuguese Passage in the *Farça de Inês Pereira* of Gil Vicente." *MLN*, 63 (1948), 342-46.

Asensio, Eugenio. "El *Auto dos Quatro Tempos* de Gil Vicente." *RFE*, 33 (1949), 350-75.

———. "El soneto 'No me mueve, mi Dios...' y un auto vicentino inspirados en Santa Catalina de Siena." *RFE*, 34 (1950), 125-36.

———. "Las fuentes de las *Barcas* de Gil Vicente: lógica intelectual e imaginación dramática." *BHTP*, 4 (1953), 207-37.

———. *Poética y realidad en el cancionero peninsular de la Edad Media*. Madrid: Gredos, 1957.

Atkinson, William C. "*Comédias*, *Tragicomédias* and *Farças* in Gil Vicente." *BdF*, 11 (1950), 268-80.

Bataillon, Marcel. *Erasmo y España*. Trans. Antonio Alatorre. 2 vols. Mexico: Fondo de Cultura Económica, 1950.

Beau, Albin Eduard. *Estudos*. 2 vols. Coimbra: Acta Universitatis Conimbrigensis, 1959.

———. "Sobre el bilingüismo en Gil Vicente." *StPh*, 1 (1960), 217-24.

Bell, Aubrey F. G. *Estudos vicentinos*. Trans. António Álvaro Dória. Lisbon: Imprensa Nacional, 1940.

———. *Gil Vicente*. Oxford: Oxford Univ. Press, 1921.

———. *Portuguese Literature*. Oxford: Oxford Univ. Press, 1922.

———. *Studies in Portuguese Literature*. Oxford: Oxford Univ. Press, 1914.

Bello, Andrés and Rufino J. Cuervo. *Gramática de la lengua castellana*. Buenos Aires: Anaconda, 1941. [References are to pars.].

Boccaccio, Giovanni. *Genealogie deorum gentilium libri*. Ed. Vincenzo Romano. 2 vols. Bari: G. Laterza, 1951.

Boggs, Ralph S. *Index of Spanish Folktales*. FF Communications, No. 90. Helsinki: Academia·Scientiarum Fennica, 1930.

Bowers, Fredson. "Established Texts and Definitive Editions." *PQ*, 41 (1962), 1-17.

———. *Textual and Literary Criticism*. Cambridge: Cambridge Univ. Press, 1966.

———. "Textual Criticism." *The Aims and Methods of Scholarship in Modern Languages and Literatures*. Ed. James Thorpe. New York: MLA, 1968, pp. 23-42.

———. "The Yale Folio Facsimile and Scholarship." *MP*, 53 (1955), 50-57.

Bowra, C. M. "The Songs of Gil Vicente." In his *Inspiration and Poetry*. London: McMillan, 1955, pp. 90-111.

Braamcamp Freire, Anselmo. *Vida e obras de Gil Vicente "Trovador, mestre da Balança."* 2nd ed. Lisbon: Rev. Ocidente, 1944.

Brasil, Reis. *Gil Vicente e o teatro moderno*. Lisbon: Minerva, 1965.

Cancionero castellano del siglo XV. Ed. R. Foulché-Delbosc. *NBAE*, 19 (1912), 22 (1915).

Cent nouvelles nouvelles. Ed. Paul Lacroix. Paris: G. Charpentier, 1884.

Chasca, Edmund de. "The Phonology of the Speech of the Negroes in Early Spanish Drama." *HR*, 14 (1946), 322-39.

CHAVES, PEDRO. *Rifoneiro português*. Porto: D. Barreira, 1945?
CIDADE, HERNÂNI. *Lições de cultura Luso-brasileira: épocas e estilos na literatura e nas artes plásticas*. Rio de Janeiro: Livros de Portugal, 1960.
CLARK, KENNETH. "The Young Michelangelo." *Renaissance Profiles*. Ed. J. H. Plumb. New York: Harper and Row, 1965, pp. 37-51.
CLEMENTE, ALICE R. "The Allegories of Gil Vicente." Diss. Brown Univ. 1967.
COROMINAS, JOAN. *Diccionario crítico-etimológico de la lengua castellana*. 4 vols. Bern: Francke, 1954-1957.
CORREAS, GONZALO. *Vocabulario de refranes y frases proverbiales*. Madrid, 1924.
COSTA RAMALHO, AMÉRICO DA. "Algumas observações sobre o latim de Gil Vicente." *Humanitas*, 17-18 (1965-1966), 198-210.
———. "Uma bucólica grega em Gil Vicente." *Humanitas*, 15-16 (1963-1964), 328-47.
COVARRUBIAS Y HOROZCO, SEBASTIÁN DE. *Tesoro de la lengua castellana o española*. Ed. Martín de Riquer. Barcelona: S. A. Horta, 1943.
CRAWFORD, J. P. WICKERSHAM. *Spanish Drama before Lope de Vega*. Philadelphia: Univ. of Penn. Press, 1937.
———. "The *Pastor* and the *Bobo* in the Spanish Religious Drama of the Sixteenth Century." *RR*, 2 (1911), 376-401.
———. *The Spanish Pastoral Drama*. Philadelphia: Univ. of Penn. Press, 1915.
DANTAS, JÚLIO. "O espíritu da reforma religiosa na obra de Gil Vicente." *BRAE*, 23 (1936), 267-81.
DANTE ALIGHIERI. *Il Convivio*. Ed. G. Busnelli and G. Vandelli. 2 vols. Florence: Felice le Monnier, 1964.
———. *La Divina Commedia*. Ed. Natalino Sapegno. 3 vols. Florence: Nuova Italia, 1960.
DEUTSCHMANN, OLAF. "Formules de malédiction en espagnol et en portugais." *BdF*, 10 (1949), 215-72.
Diccionario histórico de la lengua española. Madrid: Academia Española, 1933, vol. I.
DUNN, JOSEPH. *A Grammar of the Portuguese Language*. Hispanic Society of America Publications, No. 230. Washington, D. C.: National Capital Press, 1928. [References are to pars.].
ELIOT, T. S. *On Poetry and Poets*. New York: Farrar, Straus and Cudahy, 1957.
ELLIOTT, JOHN R., Jr. "The Sacrifice of Isaac as Comedy and Tragedy." *SP*, 66 (1969), 36-59.
Enciclopedia de la religión Católica. 7 vols. Barcelona: Dalmau y Jover, S. A., 1950-1956.
ENTWISTLE, WILLIAM J. *The Spanish Language: Together with Portuguese, Catalan and Basque*. London: Faber and Faber, 1936.
ENZINA, JUAN DEL. *Églogas*. Ed. Humberto López Morales. New York: Las Américas, 1963.
ERASMO. *El Enquiridion o Manual del caballero cristiano* and *La Paráclesis o Exhortación al estudio de las letras divinas* (Spanish translations of the 16th century). Ed. Dámaso Alonso and Marcel Bataillon. Madrid: Centro de Estudios Históricos. 1932.

Espinosa, Aurelio M. *Estudios sobre el español de Nuevo Méjico*. Trans. Amado Alonso and Ángel Rosenblat. 2 vols. Buenos Aires: Biblioteca de Dialectología Hispanoamericana, 1930-1946.

Farinelli, Arturo. *Italia e Spagna*. 2 vols. Turin: Fratelli Bocca, 1929.

Ferguson, George. *Signs and Symbols in Christian Art*. New York: Oxford Univ. Press, n.d.

Ferreira da Cunha, Celso. "Regularidade e irregularidade na versificação do primeiro *Auto das Barcas* de Gil Vicente." *StPh*, 1 (1960), 459-79.

Figueiredo, Fidelino de. *Caracteristicas da litteratura portuguesa*. 3rd ed. Lisbon: Livraria Clássica, 1923.

———. *Literatura portuguesa*. Rio de Janeiro: A Noite, 1941.

Frèches, Claude-Henri. *Le Théâtre neo-latin au Portugal: 1550-1745*. Paris: A. G. Nizet, 1964.

Frenk Alatorre, Margit. "Dignificación de la lírica popular en el Siglo de Oro." *AdL*, 2 (1962), 27-54.

———. "Glosas de tipo popular en la antigua lírica." *NRFH*, 12 (1958), 301-34.

Frye, Northrop. "Literary Criticism." *The Aims and Methods of Scholarship in Modern Languages and Literatures*. Ed. James Thorpe. New York: MLA, 1968, pp. 57-69.

Gallop, Rodney. *Portugal: A book of Folk-ways*. Cambridge: Cambridge Univ. Press, 1961.

Gillet, Joseph E. "Apiahá." *RPh*, 5 (1952), 316-18.

———. "Notes on the Language of the Rustics in the Drama of the Sixteenth Century." *HMPi*, I, 443-53.

———, ed. *"Propalladia" and Other Works of Bartolomé de Torres Naharro*. 4 vols. Bryn Mawr and Philadelphia: Univ. of Penn. Press, 1943-1961.

Gran Diccionario de la lengua castellana (de Autoridades). Ed. Aniceto de Pagés. 5 vols. Barcelona: Fomento Comercial del Libro, n.d.

Haight, Elizabeth Hazelton. "Apuleius and Boccaccio." In her *More Essays on Greek Romances*. New York: Longmans, Green and Co., 1945, pp. 113-41.

———. *Apuleius and His Influence*. New York: Longmans, Green and Co., 1927.

Hanssen, Federico. *Gramática histórica de la lengua castellana*. Halle: Niemeyer, 1913. [References are to pars.].

Hart, Thomas R. "Courtly Love in Gil Vicente's *Don Duardos*." *RomN*, 2 (1961), 103-06.

———. "Gil Vicente's *Auto de la sibila Casandra*." *HR*, 26 (1958), 35-51.

———. "La estructura dramática del *Auto de Inês Pereira*." *NRFH*, 18 (1965-1966), 160-65.

———. "The Dramatic Unity of Gil Vicente's *Comédia de Rubena*." *BHS*, 46 (1969), 97-108.

Hendrix, William Samuel. *Some Native Comic Types in the Early Spanish Drama*. Ohio State Univ. Contributions in Languages and Literatures, No. 1. Columbus: Ohio State Univ. Press, 1925.

Henríquez Ureña, Pedro. *El español en Santo Domingo*. Buenos Aires: Biblioteca de Dialectología Hispanoamericana, 1940.

———. *La versificación irregular en la poesía castellana*. Madrid: Centro de Estudios Históricos, 1933.

HERRERA, FERNANDO DE. *Poesías*. Ed. Vicente García de Diego. Madrid: Espasa-Calpe, 1914.
HESS, RAINER. "Die Naturauffassung Gil Vicentes." *Aufsätze zur Portugiesischen Kulturgeschichte*, 5 (1965), 1-64.
HIGHET, GILBERT. *The Classical Tradition*. London: Oxford Univ. Press, 1949.
The Hundred Tales. Trans. R. H. Robbins. New York: Crown Publishers, 1960.
JOINER, VIRGINIA and EUNICE JOINER GATES. "Proverbs in the Works of Gil Vicente." *PMLA*, 57 (1942), 57-73.
KEATES, LAURENCE. *The Court Theatre of Gil Vicente*. Lisbon: privately printed, 1962.
KELLER, JOHN ESTEN. *Motif-Index of Mediaeval Spanish Exempla*. Knoxville: Univ. of Tenn. Press, 1959.
KENISTON, HAYWARD. *The Syntax of Castilian Prose: The Sixteenth Century*. Chicago: Univ. of Chicago Press, 1937. [References are to pars.].
KENYON, HERBERT A. "Color Symbolism in Early Spanish Ballads." *RR*, 6 (1915), 327-40.
LANCHETAS, RUFINO. *Gramática y vocabulario de las obras de Gonzalo de Berceo*. Madrid: Sucesores de Rivadeneira, 1900.
LAPESA, RAFAEL. *Historia de la lengua española*. 5th ed. Madrid: Escelicer, 1959.
———. "La lengua de la poesía épica en los cantares de gesta y en el romancero viejo." *AdL*, 4 (1964), 5-24.
———. *La trayectoria poética de Garcilaso*. Madrid: Rev. de Occidente, 1948.
LEARNED, ERMA. *Old Portuguese Vocalic Finals; Phonology and Orthography of Accented -ou, -eu, -iu and -ao, -eo, -io*. Baltimore: Linguistic Society of America, 1950. [References are to pars.].
LEGENTIL, GEORGES. "Les thèmes de Gil Vicente dans les moralités, sotties et farces françaises." *Hommage à Ernest Martinenche: Études hispaniques et américaines*. Paris: Editions d'Artrey, n.d., pp. 156-74.
LEGENTIL, PIERRE. *La poésie lyrique espagnole et portugaise a la fin du Moyen Age*. 2 vols. Rennes: Plihon, 1949-1953.
———. "Notes sur les compositions lyriques du théâtre de Gil Vicente." *Mélanges d'histoire du théâtre du Moyen-Age et de la Renaissance (offerts a Gustave Cohen)*. Paris: Nizet, 1950, pp. 249-60.
LEITE DE VASCONCELLOS, J. *Textos arcaicos*. Lisbon: Teixeira, 1922.
LIDA DE MALKIEL, MARÍA ROSA. *Juan de Mena, poeta del prerrenacimiento español*. Mexico: NRFH, 1950.
———. "La hipérbole sagrada en la poesía castellana del siglo XV." *RFH*, 8 (1946), 121-30.
———. "La tradición clásica en España." *NRFH*, 5 (1951), 183-223.
———. "Para la génesis del *Auto de la sibila Casandra*." In her *Estudios de literatura española y comparada*. Buenos Aires: EUDEBA, 1966, pp. 157-72.
LIHANI, JOHN. "Personal Elements in Gil Vicente's *Auto Pastoril Castellano*." *HR*, 37 (1969), 297-303.
LIVERMORE, H. V. *A History of Portugal*. Cambridge: Cambridge Univ. Press, 1947.
LLORÉNS, E. L. *La negación en español antiguo. Con referencias a otros idiomas*. Madrid: Centro de Estudios Históricos, 1929.

LOVETT, GABRIEL H. "The Churchman in the Spanish Drama before Lope de Vega." *BCom,* 4 (Fall 1952), 10-13.
MÂLE, ÉMILE. *L'art religieux du XIIIe siècle en France.* Paris: Armand Colin, 1925.
MALKIEL, YAKOV. "Latin *iactāre, dēiectāre,* and *ēiectāre* in Ibero-Romance." *BdF,* 10 (1949), 201-14.
MARTÍNEZ DE TOLEDO, ALFONSO. *El Arcipreste de Talavera.* Ed. Lesley Byrd Simpson. Berkeley: Univ. of Calif. Press, 1939.
MARTÍNEZ TORNER, EDUARDO. *Lírica hispánica: Relaciones entre lo popular y lo culto.* Madrid: Castalia, 1966.
MENDES DOS REMÉDIOS, JOAQUIM. *O sentimento religioso, o sentimento patriótico, e o espírito da raça nos autos de Gil Vicente.* Coimbra: Coimbra Editora, 1923.
MENÉNDEZ PIDAL, RAMÓN, ed. *Flor nueva de romances viejos.* 20th ed. Madrid: Espasa-Calpe, 1965.
―――. *La lengua de Cristóbal Colón.* Madrid: Espasa-Calpe, 1942.
―――. *Manual de gramática histórica española.* 11th ed. Madrid: Espasa-Calpe, 1962. [References are to pars.].
―――. *Reliquias de la poesía épica española.* Madrid: Espasa-Calpe, 1951.
MENÉNDEZ Y PELAYO, MARCELINO. *Antología de poetas líricos castellanos.* Madrid: Librería de Hernando, 1898, VII, clxiii-ccxxv.
―――. *Bibliografía hispano-latina clásica.* Ed. Enrique Sánchez Reyes. Santander: Aldus, I (1950), VIII (1952).
―――. *Orígenes de la novela. NBAE,* 1 (1905), 21 (1915).
MEREDITH, JOSEPH A. *Introito and Loa in the Spanish Drama of the Sixteenth Century.* Philadelphia: Univ. of Penn. Press, 1928.
MICHAËLIS DE VASCONCELOS, CAROLINA. "Miscelas etimológicas." *HMPi,* III, 441-73.
―――. *Notas vicentinas.* Lisbon: Rev. Ocidente, 1949.
MONTEVERDI, ANGELO. "Bilinguismo letterario." *BdF,* 19 (1960), 87-93.
MORAIS SILVA, ANTÓNIO DE. *Grande Dicionário da língua portuguesa.* Ed. Augusto Moreno et al. 10th ed. 12 vols. Lisbon: Confluência, 1949-1954.
MORLEY, S. GRISWOLD. "Strophes in the Spanish Drama before Lope de Vega." *HMPi,* I, 505-31.
MÚRIAS DE FREITAS, MARIA CONSTANÇA. "A expressão da dor no *Cancioneiro Geral* de Garcia de Resende." *BdF,* 10 (1949), 287-95.
NEMÉSIO, VITORINO. *Gil Vicente: Floresta de enganos.* Lisbon: Inquérito, 1941.
NOGUEIRA-MARTINS, CARLOS. "A propósito de la *Humanidade e grandeza do Velho da Horta." RomN,* 8 (1966), 96-97.
NORTON, F. J. *Printing in Spain: 1501-1520.* Cambridge: Cambridge Univ. Press, 1966.
NOWELL, CHARLES E. *A History of Portugal.* New York: D. Van Nostrand, 1952.
O'KANE, ELEANOR S. *Refranes y frases proverbiales españolas de la Edad Media.* Madrid: Anejos del BRAE, 1959.
ORGEL, STEPHEN. *The Jonsonian Masque.* Cambridge, Mass.: Harvard Univ. Press, 1965.
PANOFSKY, ERWIN. *Studies in Iconology.* New York: Oxford Univ. Press, 1939.
PARKER, A. A. "The Approach to the Spanish Drama of the Golden Age." *TDR,* 4 (1959), 42-59.

PARKER, JACK HORACE. *Gil Vicente*. New York: Twayne, 1967.
———. "Gil Vicente: A Study in Peninsular Drama." *Hispania*, 36 (1953), 21-25.
PATCH, HOWARD R. *The Goddess Fortuna in Mediaeval Literature*. Cambridge, Mass.: Harvard Univ. Press, 1927.
PENNEY, CLARA LOUISA. *List of Books Printed before 1601 — in the Library of the Hispanic Society of America*. New York: Hispanic Society of America, 1929.
PICCUS, JULES. "El traductor español de *De Genealogia Deorum*." In *Homenaje a Rodríguez-Moñino*. Madrid: Castalia, 1966, II, 59-75.
PIEL, JOSEPH M. *Miscelânea de etimologia portuguesa e galega*. Coimbra: Acta Universitatis Conimbrigensis, 1953.
PINTO DE CARVALHO, A. "Um equívoco de Gil Vicente: Análise de um passo do *Auto da Alma*." BHS, 27 (1950), 33-36.
POPPA, ENZIO DI. "Gil Vicente compiuto poeta." *Convivium* (1952), pp. 216-32.
PORQUERAS MAYO, ALBERTO. "Nuevas aportaciones al topos 'no haber nacido' en la literatura española." *Segismundo*, 3 (1967), 63-73.
PRATT, ÓSCAR DE. *Gil Vicente: Notas e comentários*. Lisbon: Teixeira, 1931.
RABANUS MAURUS. *Allegoriae in Sacram Scripturam*. In *Patrologia Latina*. Ed. J.-P. Migne. Paris: Garnier, 1878, CXII.
RECKERT, STEPHEN. "El verdadero texto de la *Copilaçam* vicentina de 1562." *StPh*, 3 (1963), 53-68.
Refranero clásico español y otros dichos populares. Ed. Felipe C. R. Maldonado. Madrid: Taurus, 1960.
RÉVAH, I. S. "Édition critique de l'*Auto de Inês Pereira*." BHTP, 3 (1952), 196-265, 4 (1953), 75-119, 239-90, 5 (1954), 227-323.
———. "Gil Vicente a-t-il été le fondateur du théâtre portugais?" BHTP, 1 (1950), 153-85.
———. "La *comédia* dans l'œuvre de Gil Vicente." BHTP, 2 (1951), 1-39.
———. "L'*Auto de la Sibylle Cassandre* de Gil Vicente." HR, 27 (1959), 167-93.
———. *Les sermons de Gil Vicente: en marge d'un opuscule du professeur Joaquim de Carvalho*. Lisbon, 1949.
———. *Recherches sur les œuvres de Gil Vicente, I: Édition critique du premier "Auto das Barcas"*. Lisbon: Institut Français au Portugal, 1951.
———. "Un tema de Torres Naharro y de Gil Vicente." NRFH, 7 (1953), 417-25.
RILEY, E. C. *Cervantes's Theory of the Novel*. Oxford: Clarendon Press, 1962.
RIVERS, ELIAS L. "The Unity of *Don Duardos*." MLN, 76 (1961), 759-66.
ROJAS, FERNANDO DE. *La Celestina*. Ed. Julio Cejador y Frauca. Madrid: Espasa-Calpe, 1963.
Romancero general ó Colección de romances castellanos. Ed. Agustín Durán. BAE, 10 (1849), 16 (1851).
ROSSI, GIUSEPPE CARLO. "Il problema dei testi di Gil Vicente." *Filologia Romanza*, 2 (1956), 314-23.
———. *Storia della letteratura portoghese*. Florence: Sansoni, 1953.
RUIZ, JUAN. *Libro de buen amor*. Ed. Julio Cejador y Frauca. Madrid: Espasa-Calpe, 1963.
RUSKIN, JOHN. *Modern Painters*. 5 vols. Boston: Dana Estes, 1856?
SACKS, NORMAN P. *The Latinity of Dated Documents in the Portuguese Territory*. Philadelphia: Univ. of Penn. Press, 1941.

SAID ALI, MANOEL. *Grammática histórica da língua portugueza.* São Paulo: Comp. Melhoramentos de São Paulo, 1931? (2nd. ed. enlarged with a differently paginated section: *Formação de palavras e syntaxe do portuguez histórico*).

SARAIVA, ANTÓNIO JOSÉ. *Gil Vicente e o fim do teatro medieval.* 2nd ed. Lisbon: Europa-América, 1965.

——. *História da cultura em Portugal.* 3 vols. Lisbon: Jornal do Fôro, 1950-1962.

SARTON, GEORGE. "Aristotle and Phyllis." *Isis,* 14 (1930), 8-19.

SAVIOTTI, GINO. "Gil Vicente poeta cómico." *BHTP,* 2 (1951), 181-211.

SCHACK, ADOLFO FEDERICO. *Historia de la literatura y del arte dramático en España.* Trans. Eduardo de Mier. Madrid: Escritores castellanos, 1885, I.

SCHEVILL, FERDINAND. *The Medici.* New York: Harper and Row, 1960.

SEZNEC, JEAN. *The Survival of the Pagan Gods: The Mythological Tradition and its Place in Renaissance Humanism and Art.* Trans. Barbara F. Sessions. New York: Harper and Row, 1961.

SHERGOLD, N. D. *A History of the Spanish Stage from Medieval Times Until the End of the Seventeenth Century.* Oxford: Clarendon Press, 1967.

SLETSJÖE, LEIF. "Dos fenómenos lingüísticos en la obra dramática de Gil Vicente: Diptongo *oi* por *ou*; desinencia verbal *-ade*." *RJ,* 17 (1966), 301-22.

——. "Los posesivos *nuesso* y *vuesso* en el español de Gil Vicente." *RJ,* 16 (1965), 274-89.

——. *O elemento cénico em Gil Vicente.* Lisbon: Casa Portuguesa, 1965.

SPITZER, LEO. "Salmantino en *íteles* y *véntiles*." *RFH,* 8 (1946), 130-32.

——. "The Artistic Unity of Gil Vicente's *Auto da Sibila Casandra*." *HR,* 27 (1959), 56-77.

STEGAGNO PICCHIO, LUCIANA. "*Arremedilho.* Di un presunto componimento drammatico giullaresco alle origini del teatro portoghese." *AION-SR,* 2 (1960), 31-45.

——. "Diavolo e inferno nel teatro di Gil Vicente." *AION-SR,* 1 (1959), 31-39.

——. "Il *Pater Noster* dell' *Auto do Velho da Horta*." *AION-SR,* 3 (1961), 191-98.

——. "Osservazioni sull'uso di alcuni termini nell'antico teatro portoghese." *BdF,* 19 (1960), 131-43.

——. "Questioni gilvicentine." *CN,* 19 (1959), 265-74.

——. *Storia del teatro portoghese.* Rome: Ateneo, 1964.

STEN, HOLGER. "Gil Vicente et la théorie de l'art dramatique." *Études Romanes dédiées à Andreas Blinkenberg.* Copenhagen: Munksgaard, 1963, pp. 209-19.

STERN, CHARLOTTE. "Some New Thoughts on the Early Spanish Drama." *BCom,* 18 (Spring 1966), 14-19.

SWAHN, JAN-ÖJVIND. *The Tale of Cupid and Psyche.* Lund: CWK Gleerup, 1955.

TAVANI, GIUSEPPE. "Gil Vicente e il teatro medievale." *Anuario de estudios medievales,* 3 (1966), 570-73.

TEYSSIER, PAUL. *La langue de Gil Vicente.* Paris: Klincksieck, 1959.

THOMPSON, STITH. *Motif-Index of Folk-Literature.* FF Communications, Nos. 106-109, 116-117. Helsinki: Academia Scientiarum Fennica, 1932-1936.

TIRSO DE MOLINA. *Comedias.* Ed. Emilio Cotarelo y Mori. *NBAE*, 4 (1906), 9 (1907).
———. *El vergonzoso en palacio. El burlador de Sevilla.* Ed. Américo Castro. Madrid: Espasa-Calpe, 1922.
TOMLINS, JACK E. "Una nota sobre la clasificación de los dramas de Gil Vicente." *DHR*, 3 (1964), 115-31, 4 (1965), 1-16.
VALBUENA, ÁNGEL. *Literatura dramática española.* Barcelona: Labor, 1950.
VALDÉS, ALFONSO DE. *Diálogo de Mercurio y Carón.* Ed. José F. Montesinos. Madrid: Espasa-Calpe, 1947.
VALDÉS, JUAN DE. *Diálogo de doctrina christiana y El salterio traducido del hebreo en romance castellano.* Ed. Domingo Ricart. Mexico: Univ. Nacional de México, 1964.
———. *Diálogo de la lengua.* Ed. José F. Montesinos. Madrid: Espasa-Calpe, 1964.
VICENTE, GIL. *Comedia del viudo.* Ed. Alonso Zamora Vicente. Lisbon: Centro de Estudos Filológicos, 1962.
———. *Comédia de Rubena.* Ed. Giuseppe Tavani. Rome: Ateneo, 1965.
———. *Il pranto de Maria Parda.* Ed. Luciana Stegagno Picchio. Naples: Instituto Universitario Orientale, 1963.
———. *Líricas.* Ed. João de Almeida Lucas. Lisbon: Livraria Clássica, 1943.
———. *Obras.* Ed. Mendes dos Remédios. 3 vols. Coimbra: França Amado, 1907-1914.
———. *Obras completas.* Ed. Álvaro Júlio da Costa Pimpão. Barcelos: Editora do Minho, 1956.
———. *Obras completas.* Ed. Marques Braga. 2nd ed. 6 vols. Lisbon: Sá da Costa, 1951.
———. *Obras completas de Gil Vicente: Reimpressão "fac-similada" da edição de 1562.* Lisbon: Biblioteca Nacional, 1928.
———. *Obras dramáticas castellanas.* Ed. Thomas R. Hart. Madrid: Espasa-Calpe, 1962.
———. *O velho da horta.* Ed. João de Almeida Lucas. Lisbon: Ocidente, 1943.
———. *Poesía.* Ed. Thomas R. Hart. Salamanca: Anaya, 1965.
———. *Poesías de Gil Vicente.* Ed. Dámaso Alonso. Mexico: Seneca, 1940.
———. *Teatro.* Trans. Enzio di Poppa Vólture. 2 vols. Florence: Sansoni, 1957.
———. *Teatro y poesía.* Ed. Concha de Salamanca. Madrid: Aguilar, 1946.
———. *Tragicomedia de Amadís de Gaula.* Ed. T. P. Waldron. Manchester: Manchester Univ. Press, 1959.
———. *Tragicomedia de Don Duardos.* Ed. Dámaso Alonso. Madrid: Consejo Superior de Investigaciones Científicas, 1942, Ia.
———. *Tragicomédia pastoril da Serra da Estrela.* Ed. Álvaro Júlio da Costa Pimpão. Coimbra: Atlântida, 1963.
VINAVER, EUGÈNE. *Form and Meaning in Medieval Romance.* Modern Humanities Research Association, 1966.
WARDROPPER, BRUCE W. "Approaching the Metaphysical Sense of Gil Vicente's Chivalric Tragicomedies." *BCom*, 16 (Spring 1964), 1-9.
———. "*El Burlador de Sevilla*: A Tragedy of Errors." *PQ*, 36 (1957), 61-71.
WEBBER, EDWIN J. "*Arte mayor* in the Early Spanish Drama." *RPh*, 5 (1951), 49-60.

WEBER DE KURLAT, FRIDA. "Gil Vicente y Diego Sánchez de Badajoz: A propósito del *Auto da Sebila Casandra* y de la *Farsa del juego de cañas*." *Filología*, 9 (1963), 119-62.

———. "Sobre el negro como tipo cómico en el teatro español del siglo XVI." *RPh*, 17 (1963), 380-91.

WILKINS, ERNEST HATCH. "The Genealogy of the Editions of the *Genealogia deorum*." *MP*, 17 (1919), 425-38.

———. *The University of Chicago Manuscript of the "Genealogia Deorum Gentilium" of Boccaccio*. Chicago: Univ. of Chicago Press, 1927.

WILLIAMS, EDWIN B. *From Latin to Portuguese*. 2nd ed. Philadelphia: Univ. of Penn. Press, 1962. [References are to pars.]

———. "Old Portuguese *-eo*: A Note on the History of Portuguese Orthography." *BdF*, 11 (1950), 61.

WILLIAMS, RONALD BOAL. *The Staging of Plays in the Spanish Peninsula Prior to 1555*. Univ. of Iowa Studies in Spanish Language and Literature, No. 5. Iowa City: Univ. of Iowa, 1935.

WIND, EDGAR. *Art and Anarchy*. New York: Alfred A. Knopf, 1964.

WOOLF, ROSEMARY. "The Effect of Typology on the English Mediaeval Plays of Abraham and Isaac." *Speculum*, 32 (1957), 805-25.

The Department of Romance Studies Digital Arts and Collaboration Lab at the University of North Carolina at Chapel Hill is proud to support the digitization of the North Carolina Studies in the Romance Languages and Literatures series.

www.ingramcontent.com/pod-product-compliance
Lightning Source LLC
Chambersburg PA
CBHW030237240426
43663CB00037B/1234